My Schizophrenia
One Man's Struggle With Mental Illness

JOHN U. GUNTER

JoGun Publishers
Clyde, Texas

JOHN U. GUNTER

ISBN: 0692812261
ISBN-13: 978-0692812266 (JoGun Publishers)

JOHN U. GUNTER

DEDICATION

To Amanda Lyn Turner,
For whom my life is an open book.

CONTENTS

ACKNOWLEDGMENTS

I would like to acknowledge some of the people who have been there for me through some rough times in my sickness. All the people mentioned have made a difference in my life in one way or another, whether it was through treatment, bringing me to get help for my mental disorder, walking and talking with me during intense moments of mania, or writing me letters. I would have to write a whole book of acknowledgments to give everyone a thank you, but here are a few who made a difference in my mentality and some who continue to help me survive my illness with dignity and respect.

I would first like to say thank you to my father Donald Mark Gunter. He picked me up repeatedly and brought me to the doctors in the worst conditions over the years. He still supports me to this day and helps me realize my goals. I don't know what I'd do without him.

Next, my mother, Barbara Sue Claxton. She stood by me when I was a youth and has seen my disease progress over the years. She took me to the shelter and didn't abandon me when I did not at first succeed.

My sister, Mary Faith Parnell, has been a Godsend. I know she never stopped loving me and she took me in more times than I can count. I visit her often and love her family dearly. Her husband, Chris Parnell, has always treated me like a brother; her son, Devon Necessary, is my buddy and her daughter, Jade Parnell, is a character that I adore.

My brother, Joshua Mark Gunter, and I were close

as children. He remembers a lot more of my childhood than I do and every now and then I think his memory is a little flawed about how things were with me, but he always wrote to me when I was in prison, before anyone else did, and I hope to be able to do many things with him as the year's progress.

My step-sister, Amy Gray, took me in several times over the years. Although I'm not close to Amy as of this writing, I think of her a lot because I wish that I could have been better when I did have a chance to be part of her life.

My son, Johnny Mark Gunter—during the years of my untethered illness, I was not a good father to Johnny. I wasn't there when he needed me and I was distant even when I was there. Johnny loves me and today he tells me so frequently. He and his girlfriend, Josephina Sanchez, welcome me in their lives and in the lives of my granddaughters, Gabriella and Adrianna. I feel like I have another chance at being a good father and role model. My son's acceptance of me makes me feel like I've become a better person.

My daughter, Angel Marie Gunter, always made an effort with me. She always showed me she loved me. She has been a beacon in the fog many times for me. I'm extremely proud of her and will never cease to dream up ways I can one day contribute more to her life. Those thoughts keep me going when nothing else will.

There have been people during my incarceration and afterwards who were there for me and whom I would like to acknowledge:

Brian Edwards would talk to me for hours sometimes, helping me work through subjects. He tolerated my daily pacing for hours with seldom a complaint. I don't think he could have been a better friend.

Trenton Lee Wallace had a great sense of humor and we used to talk about all kinds of things that put me in a good mood.

David Doughtery liked to talk with me about our families. I know that David believed I would achieve my goals and was always a supportive friend.

Brian Parker has been a close friend. Always positive and helpful. He helped me out of advanced psychosis and helped me keep up with my medication. In the situation I was in, I don't know that I would have done as well without him. He may have literally saved my life.

Dr. M. M. Lefever is one of the most driven people I have ever met. I believe that she genuinely wants to do what is right. She helped me maintain my medications and structure. The Residential Drug Abuse Program (RDAP) at Beaumont Federal Prison and the strict way she ran it changed my life. She was the staple. The program was about much more than drug abuse and it was worth the time and effort.

The staff at Phoenix counseling services in Fort Worth, Texas, particularly Linda and 'Dottie', were there to help and they did. My counseling sessions with Linda were extremely beneficial and she loved to hear about my goals and encourage me. The group sessions with Dottie were fun and educational. She knew how to gain confidence in the participants and was an insightful person to say the least.

Connie Massey is a great person. She encourages me in every way and has proven herself a stern but understanding person. I enjoy my visits with her. The kind of support she shows me is inspirational. Mrs.

Massy was the first person to buy my first book, *Drugs, Sex & Death Toll*. Her words of encouragement regarding my work will stay with me forever.

Jacob Kinkade, of Kinkade Family Services, counseled me through some rough times and liked to challenge and validate me. He is one of the more solid people I've met in my lifetime. There will always be a special place for Jacob in my mind and heart. Although he was always professional, he is considered a dear friend to me.

Last, but definitely not least, Amanda Lyn Turner, Athena Batistatos, Darby Brewer, and Whitney Lewis. These women have been there for me more than they probably know. They are cherished to me and have been companions when the darkness of the world seemed to envelop me.

To everyone who has been a part of my life that has not been mentioned by name, thank you for helping me become the person I am today.

~ John U. Gunter
Clyde, Texas

1 INTRODUCTION

This book is based on true accounts of my life with schizoaffective disorder, bipolar type with psychosis. I was formally diagnosed with the disease about a decade prior to the time of this writing, having suffered the illness undiagnosed for decades prior to that. Both before and after my diagnosis I experienced many life-altering changes and severe mental disturbances. I write this now to shed light on life with schizophrenia/schizoaffective disorder from my viewpoint.

In the pages that follow, I'll walk you through the hell that my disease has wrought in my life, revealing how I have benefited from my experiences and even to some degree from the disease itself. This will be a very personal account of my own experiences with the illness. There are plenty of existing resources from which you may be able to gain insight and draw conclusions about this disorder. Many of them may not give you an accurate, intimate understanding about a person like me who is afflicted with it.

I'm not a doctor, I'm a patient. I have gone through years of counseling and I have a stronger grasp of reality now, and of what it means to function as a member of society, than I ever had before. I write this with the hope that it may help the reader to understand something of what it means to be mentally ill from the perspective of the mentally ill person.

There have been many heroes and heroines in my life. Although I spent most of my youth as a degenerate thug, there were family, friends, doctors, counselors, paramedics, hospital staff and even, on occasion, law enforcement officers who have tried to help me by admitting me to mental hospitals instead of cold jail cells or releasing me to a life of delusion on the streets. When I look back at all I've been through and where I am today, I don't know how I could thank them all, except to use my passion for writing to elaborate on my life and condition. Perhaps these pages will resonate with someone in need or give a better understanding of the disease to those who seek it.

Schizophrenia—*n. mental disease marked by the breakdown in the relation between thoughts, feelings, and actions, frequently accompanied by delusions and retreat from society. (The Oxford Dictionary and Thesaurus, Third Edition)*

Schizoaffective disorder is schizophrenia with manic or depressive bouts.

Hallucinations, delusions, disorganized thinking, manic behavior and depressed mood are some of the symptoms. Per the National Alliance on Mental Illness (NAMI) schizoaffective disorder is seen in about 0.3% of the population. Men and women experience the disorder at the same rate, but often the disease shows up at an earlier age in men

---

Schizoaffective disorder differs from schizophrenia. People who are schizoaffective are often misdiagnosed as either schizophrenic or bipolar. This was the case with me. My disease manifested progressively and it has now developed to the point that I lose the ability to think clearly within twenty-four to forty-eight hours of being off of my medications. When that happens, I am seized by a period of intense mania, which is only a prelude to the onset of auditory and visual hallucinations. I see and hear strange things; my existence can easily become a waking nightmare.

Although the exact cause of schizoaffective disorder is unknown, there are a few recognized triggers or contributing factors for this disorder, including 1) brain chemistry, 2) genetics, 3) drug use and 4) stressful events[1]. All four of these conditions contributed to the onset of my illness. Of course, there are plenty of people who experience but few of

[1] "Schizoaffective Disorder", National Alliance On Mental Illness, accessed August 28, 2016, http://www.nami.org/Learn-More/Mental-Health-Conditions/Schizoaffective-Disorder, Overview: Causes

these catalysts and suffer the same ailments as I. The suffering of schizoaffective symptoms is very real to the affected. I have bouts of mania and still hear a voice in my head even when properly medicated and abstinent of illicit drug use. With proper medication and rest, it's rare that I hallucinate severely.

If you have suffered from this illness, or know someone who may be suffering from it, help can be found. Without proper treatment, a person may do things to jeopardize their life and freedom without realizing what is happening to them. In the extremities of the illness, a patient's judgment is severely impaired.

If you are a student of psychology, suffer the illness, or know someone who may be suffering, the things I will tell here about my own experience may be of value to you. I believe that all of this has happened to me, in part, so that I could reach out beyond these pages and communicate my experience to you. I'm grateful for everything I have been through and survived. I'm grateful for my family. If it were not for the thought of them and their help I may not have made it through. Much of what I have to tell here is really rough stuff, and the telling of it is not easy for me, but I don't tell you these things out of sorrow. You will see in these pages that there is triumph in the trials and that there is no one to truly blame for the warped mentality of the mentally ill. How does one stop the turmoil? I will tell you what worked for me, after I outline the various symptoms and experiences that have made me who I am today.

2 SOLITARY TENDENCIES

During my childhood, I was an introvert. I don't remember having conversations often. The conversations I do remember revolved mostly around listening and learning. My great-grandfather enjoyed getting me to develop my imagination and I loved him for it. That was when I talked most. He used to enjoy asking me questions and would get a kick from hearing the fantastical ways I could come up with answering them. There were only a few people over the span of my life to date who did this with me. I've always had a vivid and creative imagination. I use it to advantage these days whenever I write fiction. I believe that my vivid imagination, mixed with a chemical imbalance in my brain, led to a lot of my problems as a schizoaffective patient.

Most of the time, I've listened. I love to learn, and listening is the best way for me to learn. I become passionate when I speak and have thoughts I wouldn't express to most people. Most of the time, I'm perfectly content being alone in my own head. I spent most of my childhood years alone. Playing alone, eating alone and—most of all—alone in my thoughts.

Being alone wasn't a sad thing for me. Remember that imagination I told you about? It always took me to new places. I would get in trouble in school for staring out of the window during class. I stayed away from home as much as possible, by myself, and never cared to join others in their games. I observed the world around me, but rarely interacted. I didn't know at the time that my imagination and solitude would become kindling for the fires of insanity.

I did find friends, but they were normally procured out of necessity and it was unusual to feel any deep attachment to anyone. I had a hard time expressing emotion towards anyone and when I made friends it revolved around having someone to walk home with, or around the fourth grade, other children to skip school and commit crimes with. I would find out later in life that I was forming unhealthy relationships and this was my habit through my grade-school, middle-school and adult years.

Being an introvert became an advantage. I could easily spot who was trouble and why they were, during my observations of the people who surrounded me. Although I found myself in quite a bit of trouble, I believe being an introvert and not getting overly attached to anyone kept me from many pitfalls. It was very easy for me to say no when I wanted to. When you simply care little about how people perceive you, it gives you a special kind of power—one that I wielded well.

You see, I set the standard for almost all of my relationships. I accepted responsibility for myself.

When troubles arose or I was in trouble, I was responsible. I either allowed people in my life for specific purposes, or I avoided them, all on my own accord. I have never submitted easily to peer pressure. Given my criminal history, you would think otherwise. I have no one to blame for my actions but myself.

The reality is that I'm a strong person internally. There are those who wouldn't think a mentally ill person is strong. The fact is that some of the qualities of schizoaffective disorder can make me stronger than others at times. Other times, I can be quite helpless to the extent that it is difficult for me to take care of myself properly on my own.

As a juvenile, when my condition worsened considerably, I could still function. Around the age of fourteen, the doctors discovered I had a chemical imbalance in my brain. They said it was the reason for my erratic behavior and violent reactions to the smallest things. They called it Bipolar Syndrome and they prescribed medications for it. I didn't believe that pills would make me better. This was because of an incident with Ritalin, which had been prescribed to me for treating Attention Deficit Disorder when I was in grade school. The Ritalin had affected my liver functions and made me sick; afterward, I was against taking medication as a cure for my mental ailments. That stance carried with me into my adult years.

My hesitation to tell people how I thought or felt made it easy to find myself alone and manic. I felt as though the only way to relieve the pressure was to run the streets. I guess all the motion and commotion kept my mind entertained enough when I didn't want to be plagued with strictly my own deranged thoughts. I acted and expanded my criminal ways. Crime became my hobby.

I say hobby because it seems like the best way to classify my behavior. I did enough wrong that I became popular in some crowds and therefore had many 'friends'. I knew better than to believe that most of these people were my real friends. We were friends because we had similar interests, but there was no deep emotional connection. There have been very few people in my lifetime who became close to me on an emotional level.

Aggression and the mentally ill person

Since a child I have been notably aggressive. I had a lot of fights throughout my lifetime, averaging 1-7 physical altercations a year since pre-school. The fights would start over petty things on most occasions. Another child may have pushed me, made fun of my clothes, hair, or just thought I was an easy target because I didn't fit in with 'the crowd'. In any case, I was a fighter. This behavior gained a lot of negative attention from teachers and parents and, as a teenager, it afforded me a reputation and helped me fit in with the element that I would embrace—fellow criminals.

Maybe if, as a teenager, I would have frequented the gym more and gone to more boxing classes, my history would have been different today than it is now. I didn't. I used my talents for fighting strictly for self-defense on the streets and I'm lucky today to have as many teeth left as I do. Of course, my front teeth have been broken and chipped in fights inside of institutions and since been fixed. Even when I won the fights, I was damaged by them.

When I feel threatened, my reaction is more

commonly *fight* rather than *flight*. The reason for this is rooted in my mental disorder. I have an overwhelming urge, a drive to neutralize people whom I perceive as a threat to my well-being. Paranoia lies behind this behavior. I become consumed with the thought that I must react to neutralize a threat or it will cause me further—even worse—problems. This paranoia has been the main catalyst in situations that turned out very physical, bloodied and bruised with violence.

I'm not proud of these things. All the fights that I remember were justified in my mind. That doesn't make them right. There were likely many times I could have been 'the bigger man' and walked away, as they say. In institutions, the concept of being 'the bigger man' goes against survival instinct. Basically, in those situations, I had to fight or be taken advantage of. It's as simple as that.

When I 'walk away' from a fight, my mind punishes me. I begin to believe that the person I failed to fight will cause bigger troubles for me in the future. The voices in my head will call me names and taunt me. I'll have vivid hallucinations due to my decision to forbear fighting—visions of the negative results that might follow. No wonder then, that in most cases throughout my life when faced with conflict I have made an example of someone, the first one to try pushing me around, everywhere I go.

Today I've learned different ways to avoid being violent. One of those ways is to avoid people and situations that put me in the position to be disrespected. I avoid criminal behavior and putting myself out there to have to defend myself behind disputes during criminal activities. I don't let *The Voice* in my head drive me. I use coping mechanisms and do my best to be a kind person.

A word about *The Voice* —I have had many hallucinations, both visual and auditory, but there has been one *Voice* that has been with me from the beginning. I trusted and often obeyed *The Voice*. I will refer to this entity as *It* or as *The Voice* in this book. I often felt *Its* presence and listened to *The Voice*. There were other voices and entities that were the subjects of my hallucinations, I'll refer to them as *they* or as *the others*. *The Voice* often warned me about what *they* would do to me or to my family—I have seen their work in visons, and it's pretty terrible stuff.

Everything becomes amplified in the schizoaffective world of mania and delusion. Medication, coupled with positive thoughts, battles most of my aggression. I find now that people on average enjoy interacting with me. Some are even pleasantly surprised at my character, compared to my looks. Being tattooed from head to ankle and weighing over 200 lbs., my appearance alone gives most people the impression that I am trouble. I'm honored when someone tells me that I'm not what they expected after having a conversation with me.

Being violent and having overwhelming negative thoughts had crippled my life for many years. I am proud of who I have become with the help of people who took the time to care about me and teach me a better way. I owe a lot of my recovery and ongoing life improvements, coping with this disease, to the groups of people I mentioned in the introduction to this book. Without them I'm sure I would be dead or would have continued down a destructive path to my death.

The attraction of drugs as a solution

My illicit drug consumption drastically increased around the time I began to experience heightened symptoms of schizophrenia/schizoaffective disorder. I had dealt with hallucinations before my drug use increased. After I started having terrible nightmares, I increased my drug use to avoid sleep.

Some difficult things happened in my family during this period—deaths and stress-driven circumstances. My marriage was on the rocks because of situations out of my control. I began to believe horrible things, and when I slept, my dreams became vivid nightmares. I began using stimulants to stay up longer and avoid the nightmares. This only increased my visions and auditory hallucinations while awake. At first I was okay with that, because I told myself they weren't real.

Attempting to ignore the hallucinations only worked briefly, because eventually, everybody must sleep. I became consumed in a world of delusion that eventually led to my divorce and years of homelessness. Once I had let my mind reach the point of constant insanity, the illicit drugs didn't help. They only served to make my mentality worse. At that time, I lived in a world of constant chaos. Visual and auditory hallucinations became my life. Not only did I suffer mental illness naturally, I induced a higher state of insanity by becoming a drug addict.

So, I became a drug addict by design, and I was very much a mentally unstable person. These things put me on the radar with the police and kept me shunned by people who did not use drugs or attempt to understand my dilemma. My perception of reality became so distorted that most people assumed I was on drugs or intoxicated, even when I was sober. I was arrested multiple times for public intoxication, when I hadn't had a drink. I understood I was being arrested, but my inability to communicate properly led the officers to believe I was intoxicated.

I don't blame them. I froze up in the middle of the street on one occasion and couldn't make myself respond when they tried talking to me. It's no one's fault. Not theirs, not mine. At that time in history, I had yet to be diagnosed. I can't expect that anyone would automatically assume what was going on with me. I didn't even know what was wrong with myself.

I kept using drugs and living in the streets for many years. I had gotten so bad that no one wanted me in their homes. Think about it. I would be away from most people for long periods of time and then show up in poor condition. They thought I was a junkie.

The worst part about it is that most people were quick to turn me away, drop me off somewhere away from them, or offer me a dose of methamphetamine or some other drug. People offered me drugs more often than they offered me a plate of food. Truth is, I probably did less than two or three grams a month when I lived on the streets, for many years, before my diagnosis.

I rarely purchased drugs when I was homeless, but I didn't turn them down often either. I wanted to get 'on my feet' and live better, but I didn't know how. I was overwhelmed with my mental disorder and rarely functioned at my full potential. No one could save me. I was in and out of hospitals and wouldn't tell the doctors what was going on with me. I didn't want to be sick. I wanted to believe it was the drugs. I wanted to believe that my problems would go away on their own. On top of that, *The Voice* told me not to tell anyone what was happening with me. *It* said that *the others* would kill my family and friends, and I believed it.

Drugs were my method, my excuse. I didn't want to face the fact that, although my condition improved when I was sober, it never went away. It never has. I struggle daily, and the only thing that has changed me enough to live a somewhat normal life now is behavioral therapy, psychotherapy, medication and coping skills.

When there is someone to be with

My relationship with my wife is what held me together as a young adult, before extreme circumstances brought an end to the relationship. My ex-wife and I had been together since I was about fourteen or fifteen years old. She was my world and someone I could confide in. She was the girl who would eventually become the woman who was by my side. She helped me to live in a way I didn't know was possible. She made my life much more than I think it ever would have been without her.

Having someone to spend time with when you don't want to leave your room for days is a treasure. She would watch movies with me and comfort me when my paranoia immobilized me. For a mentally ill person, a companion is the ultimate medicine. Being able to trust someone with your thoughts relieves the pressure. The voices become calmer.

When the sickness takes over, life with a companion can go two ways. If the companion is receptive and listens to issues with an open mind, they can help the afflicted person overcome, but if the companion shows a lack of understanding it can become hurtful. Paranoias begin to spill over onto the companion and the relationship becomes strained.

Having a healthy relationship when either party is under duress is a lot of work. If both parties are under duress and one is mentally warped, the relationship becomes a minefield of problems. Eventually, in cases like mine, the relationship can erupt into perversions and aggression.

When the quality of life becomes unbearable, it is inevitable that there will be separation. Separation affects a mentally ill person such as myself in the same way a death does. Basically, a lifeline is gone. The life you've known up to that point is over. You mourn. Relationships with a sick person are hard to pull through. I don't blame anyone who has left me in my sickness. I know I was a difficult person to deal with. Aggressive, distant and cold.

Disconnection from family

One of the most disturbing parts of my disease was the disconnection from family in general. I didn't know how to talk to my children or enjoy doing the things I used to do with them as much. We used to go to movies and restaurants, BBQ's of friends and family and various other activities.

When my symptoms became unbearably noticeable, I started to shun the world. When they became a constant, I retreated from life as a family man altogether. I spent days in a room by myself and did not socialize. At times when I went into public, or associated with people, I didn't feel right. My world was folding in on me.

I felt apprehensive about telling anyone what was happening with me. There was some embarrassment.

I felt destroyed inside. I would lose control and found myself being filled with hatred. I hated that people treated me differently. I hated that I couldn't connect with them like I used to. I hated anyone who caused me any kind of discomfort.

My family pushed me away, and I began to believe that no one cared for me. I couldn't seem to change or fully understand the fact that I was getting sicker. Lack of communication eventually left me a shell of a human being. I could remember a time when I felt whole. I watched friends and family interact at functions I would attend and didn't understand why I couldn't be like them.

When your mentality is unstable, without diagnosis, what you present is a problem that no one seems to have the time to solve. My mind had dug a hole deep enough for me that I became an alien even to those who once knew me best. Friends, who considered themselves family, attempted to help. My actual relatives attempted to help. In my state of mind, there was little they could do for me.

I became despondent; so much so, that I began to lack basic emotions. My reflexes became random and uncommon. Mania would set in and I didn't behave like I did when I was a child or adolescent. I didn't go into the streets and work off the energy. I didn't talk to my friends and family. I stayed home and in delusion, dreaming up the plots that I thought others had devised against me.

Acting that way, my family ultimately had enough of me. They didn't want me in their homes. They didn't want me coming around. The only places of refuge left for me at that time were drug houses and alley-ways. Without the support of my family, I was done for: Doomed to an existence as a vagrant.

There were times when my family still tried to help me. Their solution was usually the hospital. I would be admitted to hospitals again and again. When I would be released, usually days later, I had nowhere to go. I hadn't spoken freely and openly to the doctors about the problems I was experiencing, and I received no more help. I'd walk for days, only to end up in the same places, wallowing in sickness.

It's not my family's fault and I blame them in no way. Once again, I didn't know what was wrong with me. The doctors had yet to diagnose me. As far as my family knew, I was just a drug addict, doing these things to myself.

What they didn't know, and I failed to reveal, was that there was something much more serious than drugs happening with me. I was listening to *The Voice*, and *It* told me not to tell anyone about my thoughts and experiences. *The Voice* insisted on silence, and not only spoke to me, but gave me visions as well. I thought I was protecting my family and friends by being silent.

I don't know how things would have been if I could have articulated my thoughts and described to someone the things I was experiencing. I don't regret my life or the way things panned out. My family is my greatest support system today—since I gained a new mindset, abstained from drug use, went to counseling, and take my medication regularly—I can only bring myself to believe that they never stopped loving me and hoping for my return from insanity, before I died in the streets or some institution. A support system is something that is priceless to a mentally ill person.

The years that I spent alienating myself from the

people closest to me were some of the worst years of my life. Sick or not, I would try unsuccessfully to make contact. I wanted to be in their lives, but I was too far gone. I know they didn't know what to think of me. I was unpredictable. No one wants to sleep with someone in the house who may be capable of anything, whose mental health is ill and strange.

The thing that hurt most about my disconnection from the ones I loved was separation from my children. For years, my relationship with my children was non-existent. I knew that my son suffered from mental illness, too. Not being able to be a part of his life and not knowing what condition he was in hurt me. My daughter, whom I love dearly, was growing up without me and every time I saw her she was changing. They were both getting older and I wasn't a part of their lives due to my condition, even when I was present.

Over time I came to realize that I wasn't getting any better. I wandered away and the only time I would see my family would be during some of my brief hospitalizations. The world was an empty place, and the people who were sometimes willing to take me in would seldom actually take care of me. There weren't three meals a day; a lot of times there was not even one. There weren't clean towels and clothes to wear. At one point, I didn't even have my own shoes. I was a man without a home and remained that way for many years.

My family was always the light at the end of my tunnel, even when they weren't able to be there for me, and more so when they were. I always thought of them and would often rack my brain on how I was going to get better. Unfortunately, before my diagnosis, I was left mainly to my own devices. Those devices were failing me miserably.

Being around others with mental illness

I have encountered countless others who are suffering from mental illness and still do to this day. My reaction is to try to help them, even if it's just with a conversation of encouragement. Kind words and encouragement always went a long way with me, so I know how much they can help. Anytime I talk to someone who is homeless and/or mentally ill, I do my best to be positive and inquire about their lives.

Most people ignore the homeless and see them as trash—I don't. I've been there. I was never in the habit of being cruel to people less fortunate than me to begin with, but once you've lived it, your perspective shifts more than a little. I know that a great majority of homeless are mentally ill. I don't think they're all lazy and worthless. I think most have serious problems functioning and they just don't know how to conduct themselves properly. I think that a large portion of the homeless have simply been written off by society.

You don't have to be a drug addict to be homeless and you don't have to be a drug addict or homeless to be insane. In my life I have lived many ways. I've had the opportunity to meet a large variety of people. I found that all people have a little craziness in them, and some have a lot of craziness.

The kind of insanity I met in the streets was what I'd call *compulsive craziness*. People out for immediate gratification. Then there were some that were *religiously insane*. Some were *criminally insane*. The rarest of all, those with my kind of insanity—*schizoaffective* sufferers—were few and far between. They were there though. It appears that, when you have the disease, you draw in people like yourself to some extent.

In hospitals, there were insane people, just like me—in a way. I couldn't say there are any two people just alike, and I always wondered if some of the patients looked at me and thought, *I'm glad I'm not that guy.* I did when I had the faculties to see anything more than my hallucinations. I saw people who couldn't take care of themselves. I didn't think I would progress to that, but eventually I did.

The shuffling, drooling, dirty kind of insanity. The worst kind. When you've reached this level, no one can help you out easily. It takes medication and therapy to start functioning normally again, and those who do come back from that abyss have done a lot of the work for themselves. You must want it. You can't completely give in or give up. The longer you wallow, the less likely it is that you will be able to eventually grasp sanity and call it yours.

Another subject I know about is *prison crazy*. There's a concentration of irrational people in prison. Some are okay, but almost all have immediate gratification issues and most are emotionally damaged, although they won't say that. I gather these things from observation. As I stated earlier in the book, I observe and listen more than anything else I do.

What I observed most about prisoners is that they are violent. They look for ways to hype things up and people to attack. Whether it's attacking others by taking what they believe belongs to them, starting rumors, or physically harming someone for the smallest offensive behaviors, they're always on the prowl. Sometimes, to live with the wolves, you must become a wolf. I adapt very well, but I find that being reserved and reluctant to express a full opinion, even when solicited, can go a long way in keeping a person out of drama.

The pill line was always full in prison. Some of the inmates needed the pills, like me. Others tried to get doctors to prescribe them drugs they could sell on the compound. Even if the person might need the prescription for himself, greed is a factor for most. I'm not sure if all those in the medication line had mental issues. I guess it doesn't matter. If they did all have issues, some were willing to forgo their medication in order to make a few bucks; willing to suffer for a honey bun.

I often thought I could see something in the eyes of some of the guys in prison. They had a sickness that I could glimpse there. Often, I was correct about them. Those with the gleam of latent insanity in their eyes usually ended up stabbing someone or in some other kind of drama. The craziness was evident in them.

Of all the craziness that I've found in all the places I've been and everything I know of insanity, I know mine the best. That's what I will go into detail about. I want to illustrate the notion that insanity is more commonplace than you would think. It's everywhere, in different severities. Some who are sick are simply not diagnosed. Others lack the drive, or the tools, or the skills to pull themselves out of the muck.

3 MY FORMAL DIAGNOSIS

Eventually, I came to a point in my life when I'd had enough. On this occasion, I was hospitalized after being found unresponsive in the dining area of a fast food restaurant. I had been hospitalized in an unresponsive condition on other occasions, but this time would be different, because this time I would ask the doctors for help.

I remember the night vividly. I remember that I had wandered up to this restaurant in a bad way. I had been walking all day and into the night. I knew I looked bad in my tattered jacket and dirty clothes.

I don't know why I was standing in front of the restaurant, frozen in place. A Jaguar drove up next to me and the driver stuck some money out of the window. I wasn't sure what to do. All my years homeless and I had never been the begging type. The man said, "Go on. Take it. I know you need to eat."

I took the money and the car drove away. I looked at the bills and thought about what I could buy. There was a dollar menu. Maybe a small burger and a water?

I heard the door open to the establishment and a man stepped out. He was a young guy. Probably early twenties. He lit a cigarette and began staring at me. I noticed he was wearing a uniform for the restaurant. I thought he was about to tell me to leave. He took a long drag off his cigarette and put it out.

Before going in, he asked, "Do you want something to eat?"

I didn't respond. I stood there with the dollar bills in my hand. The voices in my head were cruel—they told me that he would poison me. The voices told me that they were serving human meat inside. I was so hungry, but I couldn't respond verbally.

The guy said, "Come on, man. Come in, I'll hook you up."

I didn't say a word, but I followed him inside to the counter. The servers made me a meal and I tried to give them the two dollar bills. They wouldn't take them. I picked up my tray and went to sit in the dining area. I ate the meal and afterwards, I froze completely.

The Voice told me that I was a dog. I could feel myself turning into a dog. My nostrils were flaring and I felt hairs growing out of my neck, back and arms. I wanted to move. I wanted to get up and leave, but I couldn't. I couldn't make myself do anything.

The restaurant was closing and the person sweeping the floors came to me. I could hear him telling me it was time to go. I couldn't bring myself to respond or look up. People from the establishment began gathering around me and I heard one of them say they were calling the police. I tried telling myself to get up and leave, but I couldn't make myself do it.

I remember the police showing up. They were

walking around me, commenting on the tattoos they could see on me. One of them went through the pockets of my jacket that he could easily reach. Inside one of my pockets, he found a phone number to a friend. I remember hearing him make the call and describing me to whoever was on the phone. The police began having a conversation about what to do with me. Paramedics arrived and I remember an officer telling them that they could have me. I remember the paramedics sounded excited that they would get to take me.

When they wheeled me out of the restaurant, I remember how all the red and blue lights looked, flashing against the building. I felt odd, like I was a circus exhibit. I was the main attraction. *The Voice* told me the war was over. I didn't believe it and it wouldn't be the first or last time that *The Voice* lied to me.

The paramedics ran tests on me on the way to the hospital. I have vague memories of being admitted into the facility and I remember them talking about a drug overdose. They pumped my stomach and it was later confirmed that it was in fact *not* a drug overdose. I was in what they described as a mental coma.

I remember them putting food in front of me periodically for the next week. I could not bring myself to communicate with the staff or to eat. I remember being extremely hungry. I fell in and out of consciousness. I tried to tell myself to move—to eat—I stayed in that condition for about a week, until one day I reached for the food. I remember looking at my hand and forcing myself to move. I saw tracers of my hand when I achieved motion.

A nurse saw me reaching for the food and alerted

other nurses and doctors who immediately filled the room. By the end of the day, my mother was there and she had a conversation with me. I wasn't very talkative, and my motor skills were slow. She was in the room when the doctor suggested I be admitted into the psych ward, again. He said it was evident, from their observation of me the past week, that I had psychiatric issues that needed to be addressed. My mother told me that if I went to the psych ward and followed some type of program, she would be supportive. She said she would try to get me involved in my children's lives again. That was the ultimate incentive for me. I wanted badly to be part of my family's lives.

In the mental ward, I faced familiar issues. The voices called me names and told me things to disturb me. They told me not to talk to the doctors. The staff gave me extra plates of food and everyone was very kind; still I would not speak. They knew something was going on with me that I wouldn't speak of, so they kept me longer than the usual seventy-two hours for observation. A couple of weeks in, the doctors had tried to talk to me multiple times with no results. I was living in a fantasy world, in my mind. *The Voice* warned of repercussions if I spoke with the doctors about *them*.

Finally, the doctor sat across from me, and said, "Mr. Gunter. We have to release you today, unless you tell us what's happening with you."

I thought about my family again. I thought about the streets and how I'd been roaming them, wishing I could function properly, for years. I thought of all the hell the voices and hallucinations had put me through up to that point. They were going chaotic in my mind and I couldn't stop them. I didn't know if I could trust the doctor.

The Voice in my head was telling me the usual—that if I told the doctor, *the others* would kill my family. Telling me that if I told the doctor, I was betraying them. Telling me they would kill me. Telling me that if I told about the hallucinations, things would be worse, that nothing was going to be better.

It was always jarring when *they* would tell me things like that. I didn't want my family harmed. I didn't want to die. Being called traitor in my world was one of the worst things I could possibly be called. *The Voice* had kept me silent for long enough. I looked at the doctor and simply said, "I'm hearing voices and seeing things."

The doctor wrote on his pad. He said, "We can help you now, Mr. Gunter."

I was diagnosed schizoaffective with psychosis.

Living with treatment

Life being sober and medicated wasn't easy for me at first. I battle the voices constantly. When I left the hospital, my mother had researched several programs for me. I tried to be admitted to one that required sober living and they teach you a trade. I was turned away because of the types of medications I had been prescribed. I'm sure today that it was the best thing, because I doubt that in my former condition I could have completed the program.

The other program was at a homeless shelter. They wanted me to go to an in-patient drug rehab program, before I could have a resident bed in the mission program. They had a facility that they sent clients to, and I attended. I was there for a couple of weeks before I had a mental meltdown, again. I froze in a group meeting. I believed the floor was filled with snakes and I didn't want to move. I was sent back to the hospital in a non-responsive state.

Note that I hadn't been using drugs for over a month at that time and was taking my medication like I was supposed to. I experienced the heavy psychosis completely sober and medicated. I had to get a medication adjustment under hospital observation. When I was released from the hospital, I was out of the program, but I didn't wander off and get lost in the streets as usual when released. I called my mother and she talked to a friend who let me stay with him until I could get another bed in the program.

I often suffered hallucinations, but I held myself together. I went to the program and completed it. The voices didn't like my progress. They called me names and made their threats daily. I did what I could just to get by. Sometimes I contemplated suicide. I have always been firmly against suicide, but I couldn't stop the thoughts.

My mother gave me pictures of my children. One picture was of my son and daughter standing side by side. When I lived in the shelter, I looked at that picture every day. I wrote my suicide note on the back of it. Things I wanted my kids to know. I thought about ending my life often, and I would take the picture out of my back pocket, where I always kept it, to look at it. There were times I'd walked into downtown and looked at buildings and parking garages. I knew I could get to the top, and I knew the fall would kill me.

I looked at the picture several times, standing at the bottom of those buildings, and never made the trip to the top. It wasn't good enough. Leaving my children that way, no matter what the note said, it was not good enough. I knew I had to get better, and I had to be there for them. To this day I am glad I didn't write that note on a plain piece of paper.

They gave me a job at the mission, working in the kitchen. I worked thirty-two hours a week and I was grateful to have something to do. Although my motor skills were slow and I suffered fatigue at times, due to medications, I worked and enjoyed it. The staff was kind and I felt comfortable, like I belonged. It also gave me some self-respect. I wasn't just trying to lay around in the shelter, I contributed by working in the kitchen. Although the voices and visions were cruel, it helped that I had a place to be and a job to do.

They paid me fifteen dollars a week. That was fine with me. I had a bed and a shower and company. The guys at the mission were interesting to watch and some of them became my friends. Although I was quiet and moved slowly, people still liked me. For the first time in a long time, I had a place to be and people who wanted to spend time with me. I began keeping journals, a suggestion from my mother.

I went to my mental health appointments and was assigned a case worker. She was also very kind to me and didn't ask me to go into detail about the voices or visions or my life. She let me speak of what I wanted to speak of, in my own time. Eventually, it became easier to talk about my thoughts and my ailments.

I began to realize that my condition wasn't something that I had to be silent about. The more I opened up, the more willing people were to help me. After about a year and a half of making my appointments, they told me that I was eligible for social security due to my mental condition. I applied, and a few months later, I received a check. I had been at the mission for about eighteen-months and a short time after receiving the check, I made plans to move out on my own again.

Falling back into the same old traps

I decided to proposition a friend, Kenneth, and his girlfriend, Kathy, about being my roommates. I had been talking to them for over a year at that time. Kenneth used to stay in the mission with me, but the rules were strict for remaining in the residential program, so I could sympathize when he decided to leave. He and Kathy were now staying in a tent in the woods. There was another guy, James, who went into the woods to visit 'tent city' as often as I did. James had a job. I talked to Kenneth about getting an apartment together with me, Kathy and James.

We searched for a few days, eventually finding a place in a low rent complex. The apartments were small and run down; the neighborhood was a pretty undesirable area. After living in the streets for years before the mission, the prospect of having my own room and residence overruled my judgment of the company I was to keep and the neighborhood issues.

I moved into the apartment with enthusiasm and I spoke to my roommates about not getting involved with the people in the neighborhood. I wanted solitude. In my room, I was in my own world, and I spent a lot of time there alone.

One of the conditions I set with my roommates was that they each pay their portion of the rent, but I knew Kathy had issues. She was nineteen years old and had been on the streets since her eighteenth birthday. I was convinced that she needed mental health care, and didn't expect her to get a job.

Kenneth obtained employment soon after we moved in and everything was going well for the first month or so. I still had mental anxiety issues and didn't like interacting with too many people, especially people that I hardly knew. Being that way made me hesitant when time came to deal with the landlord each month. I would send my friend to pay the rent.

Kenneth had been clean from hard drugs for some time, but had been an addict before I met him at the mission. Eventually, he began talking to some of the guys in the apartments and buying drugs. When he asked to use my phone, then gave it to someone else who ran away with it, I told him to quit dealing with people in that neighborhood. If he wanted drugs, we could go to people I knew in my old neighborhood. I wanted to lower the risks of being robbed. Once I was involved and we started buying drugs from my old neighborhood, I began using again.

The problem with illicit drug use when coupled with mental illness is *amplification*. Psychotic symptoms can be greatly amplified. When you have a schizoaffective disorder, and use the types of drugs that induce psychotic symptoms in a natural subject, your condition is magnified and mental deterioration comes much faster than it does with a healthy individual.

The drugs caused me much chaos. I quit journaling. My paranoias and aggravations peaked. I became unsettled with some of the things that James was doing and it resulted in a physical altercation between us. He left the house, so rent increased. Shortly after James left, Kenneth quit his job, anticipating a settlement that Kathy was due for. The settlement came through and we split the rent for a few months.

I didn't like the lifestyle we were living and a fight broke out between Kenneth and me. I left town for the weekend and when I came home, the locks had been changed by management. When the manager let me in, I found that my apartment had been trashed; it was a disaster. Everything of value was gone, down to my bed and clothing. The worst for me were the missing journals. I had nearly two years' worth of daily writing in a stack of journals and now they were gone. My only comfort was that they must have been interesting enough for someone to steal.

The manager said that my 'friend' hadn't paid the rent in months and that I owed a lot of money. I couldn't have stayed there had I wanted to. Fortunately, I had arranged for a moving truck and could collect what little was left of my things as well as what some of the better neighbors would give back. Unfortunately, no sign of my journals.

There was a blank journal left in my room. It was disturbing, because a girl had put her first name on the front, and on the very last page was my name and a list of my medications, followed by the milligrams of each. I don't know what possessed her to do that.

I couldn't get by without a roommate, and all the candidates I knew were drug users. I ended up staying in a place where I had easy access to drugs. Eventually, I ran out of medication and neglected to go to the doctor for refills. I had another mental breakdown. My father picked me up and I was admitted into the hospital for the first time in about two years.

I was revived with the care of hospital staff once again. The doctors never seemed to judge me. The nurses always treated me kindly and with respect. I attended the in-patient program for a few weeks, then a man from a mental health group-home came to visit me. He said that if I wanted to live in one of his group-homes I could. The other option would be the state hospital.

I agreed to go to the group-home, so the man picked me up from the hospital a few days later. I rode in silence, hallucinating about the vehicle we were in, the cars beside us and the man I was riding with, they all seemed to be changing constantly. The cars would change colors in a blink of the eye, and the man's voice would change tones randomly.

It was strange being in a home full of mentally ill people. The conditions were poor and I wasn't comfortable. The residence seemed to make my symptoms worse. The longer I stayed, the more disturbed I became. I had a physical altercation with another male resident after only a few days.

I felt compelled to leave, and I did. I walked from the border of Fort Worth, Texas into Arlington, and called a friend to pick me up. I don't remember using, but I didn't have my medication. My mental faculties deteriorated quickly. The friends I was staying with got in touch with my mother and she brought me back to the hospital. It was difficult for me to believe that I couldn't function without medication. I didn't want that to be true.

After I was admitted to the care of the hospital, the man from the group-home showed up and talked to me again. He said that I still had a place in the house if I wanted it. I wanted to be out of the hospital, so I agreed to go back. I had a cell phone but hadn't powered it on in over a month. The grips of psychosis made me paranoid. I thought that, if I turned it on, it would make more voices. The service was good, but I just hadn't been able to press the power button.

After a week in the house, I turned the phone on and instantly text messages began popping up. Some were from another friend from the mission. He was telling me he had gotten an apartment with a spare bedroom. In the messages, he asked me to call him. When I called, he was glad to hear my voice. He said he'd like for me to come stay a while. I told him about my situation. I didn't want to leave the group-home in the same way I'd done before. I wanted to do it right.

I got in touch with the group-home owner and told him I wanted to leave. I told him I didn't like the living conditions and the others were driving me up the wall. He was aware of some of my altercations. The man I had fought with reported me when it happened. I don't know why I wasn't arrested. The police didn't even want to talk to me. It was still a strike with the owner. He knew I wasn't getting along.

He told me I could go, but that if I went off my meds and got hospitalized again, he wouldn't pick me up. I would be committed to the state hospital for a year, minimum. I knew I would have to stay sober, off the hard drugs that affected me so poorly, and stay on my meds—or life was going to get pretty bad. My experiences in the hospitals were miserable after a few days or weeks. They don't let you have much to entertain yourself with in there and I've never been very interested in television. Then there are the other patients—I have a hard time dealing with being around some of the patients. I'm sure I wasn't always a pleasure to some of them, either.

I packed my things and my mother picked me up. I went to live with my friend. Quality of life improved quite a bit. My friend was laid back and he didn't use hard drugs. I kept my appointments with psychologists and case workers. There were several other men from the mission on the bus line whom I could visit often, so I wasn't stuck in the house. This arrangement lasted for several months.

The thing was, although living conditions were improved and I did everything I was supposed to, my friend wasn't supposed to have anyone living with him. His case worker found out, then I was put out on my own. A lady was at an apartment I was visiting when I got the call about having to move out. She overheard the conversation and told the friend I was visiting that I could stay at her place for a couple of weeks, if I was clean and paid rent.

I agreed and went to stay with the lady. She would leave early in the morning and wanted me out of the house looking for a more permanent place while she was gone each day. When she returned in the afternoon, I was welcome to come back. This arrangement lasted for over a week, but the neighborhood was infested with criminal activity. I was no stranger to crime, and knew I couldn't afford an apartment on my own, so I began selling weed.

One thing led to another, I stayed on my meds, but ran the streets. Another friend from the mission wanted to get an apartment with me. He was about my age and we had always gotten along well. We found a place in some more low rent apartments. Everything was good there except for noise complaints from the neighbors. I had acquired a radio. I guess I didn't mention how much I love music.

Eventually some of the guys I sold weed to asked me about meth. I didn't want to touch the stuff, but they knew my history with it, and some of them knew I had been getting it for my old roommate. I knew that meth would make me more money than the weed, so before long I gave in to the temptation to deal it.

I scored a small stash, and for the first time in a while, I used some. I literally smoked one bowl before I got pulled over in my roommate's car. I was caught with less than a gram and on my way to prison for the first time since my diagnosis. I remember worrying that I would have mental issues while I was down. I didn't like the thought of that, so I rarely missed pill call. When I did, I would become manic and already be hallucinating and having abnormal thoughts by the time I made it to pill line the next day. I hardly missed more than a day, and when I did that it was usually due to a failure of the institution rather than my own neglect.

I came home after my sentence was up. This time I had a place on my sister's couch. A friend gave me a truck to drive and my father helped me get my license back. I thought I could get a job, maybe go to school and learn to drive big rigs, but that didn't work out. There were concerns about my mental state and me being behind the wheel of a heavy piece of machinery. My patience hadn't developed to the point that I could stay in one place long, if I didn't have to. Keep in mind, I always heard voices, every day I heard voices and I still do, medicated or not. I didn't get off of my meds immediately, because I knew that if I did things would turn out badly.

I took my medication like I was supposed to and things were going okay at first, but I started seeking out old friends and environs to entertain myself. I was back on social security and eventually ran into a woman who was interested in hooking up with me. She was the fast type and I began using heavily with her. While I was on my meds I didn't get too crazy, meaning the voices and hallucinations didn't take over my life.

The thing is, like I said before, when you use narcotics illegally, you tend to become neglectful of relationships and health. Since my mental health is poor, when I neglect to do what's right to keep myself balanced, things get hectic. So, I quit making doctor's appointments and ran out of meds. When I get too far out there, I have to be hospitalized, there's no communicating with me.

I did end up in the hospital and it was a recurring cycle that seemed to have no end, right up until my last incarceration. I was sentenced to the federal penitentiary for several years for possession of stolen mail. During that bid, I learned a lot about myself. I found a purpose for my life and I studied everything I could get my hands on to achieve my goals and solidify my purpose.

I decided I was going to be a writer. I'd been told several times throughout my life, since the seventh grade, that I should write books. I always blew those suggestions off. I didn't see the beauty in it. I always wrote for pleasure. I didn't visualize writing for profit and therapy as something I wanted to do. Now I began to see that writing for profit, writing for therapy and writing for pleasure are one and the same for me. It's therapeutic, whether I write fiction or non-fiction. Every minute and hour that I write is therapeutic. I'm going to tell you about my successes in this book, but first, I want to go back in time. A time before my diagnosis.

4 MY PSYCHOSIS: CATALYSTS & TRIGGERS

The mind is like a clock that is slowly running down and must be wound up daily with good thoughts. ~ Bishop Fulton J. Sheen

The first pivotal moment

The first pivotal moment of delusion and chaos came when I was stabbed at nineteen years old. Back then, I didn't do much in way of drugs; that is to say, I didn't use much. I didn't consider myself an addict. I was healthy. My dream was to be a soldier in the United States Army. I'd been putting it off because I was a new father. Food and diapers were hard to come by, so I was selling drugs and just trying to keep the household going. On my eighteenth birthday, I failed to enlist.

I've always been a car fanatic. From childhood, with Hot Wheels in the driveway, to my first auto-theft as a teenager, to owning my own rides. I had an 80's model Buick Riviera, a low-rider with a loud system and wire wheels, scrubbing the ground. The car was in good condition when I bought it. I got it cheap and it attracted a lot of attention, the wrong attention.

A group of guys set my alarm off a few days before Christmas in the late 90's. I was wrapping presents with my wife at the time. A friend was over, relaxing. When the alarm went off, I looked down into the parking lot and saw five guys in the empty parking space between my car and their truck. I didn't think about grabbing my pistol or a knife, I didn't even put my shirt on. I went down stairs to see what was going on. I had always been one of little fear. In my mind, the worst that was going to happen was getting jumped. I'd been in group fights throughout my youth and knew how to handle myself better than most. The confidence that I could give them a good fight gave me a false sense of security.

My friend and I went to the parking lot and I asked the guys what they were doing. One of them told me they were there to visit his girlfriend. I asked them to try not to set my alarm off again. They agreed. My friend and I walked away. I went to the soda machine a few feet away. I tried to put a dollar in, but it wouldn't take it. There was a girl on the pay phone next to the machine. I asked her whether she had a good dollar.

Before she could answer, my car alarm went off. The guy who had just agreed to try not to set it off was sitting on the hood. I approached him and he put his hands up in a surrender. He said he was playing. I told him I don't play like that. I turned to look for my friend and he 'hit' me in the side—at least, that's what I thought he'd done at the time. I began fighting. My first blow knocked him down and I noticed he was clutching a bloody knife. I had been stabbed.

I turned to the other four, and they began to fan out. I felt agitated and got ready to fight the group. Before any of them could get within my reach, my friend and several neighbors were there for the brawl. It was chaotic. My friend told me to go call the ambulance. He said they had my back, so I went to the pay phone that the girl had occupied. She was in the fetal position, scared by the fighting so close to her. She wouldn't give me the phone, but started screaming when I tried to take it. I wasn't in pain. I felt nothing, but I knew the knife was too long not to have done some serious damage. I went up to my apartment to make the call.

I got on the phone with emergency services. They were asking too many questions and I was anxious to get back to the fight. I was livid about being stabbed. I called my wife to handle the phone call. She also wanted to know what happened, to look at my wounds. I looked in the cabinet, at my pistol. I debated for a split second to go down and kill my assailant with the gun. I decided against that idea, but that I wasn't going to the hospital alone. I grabbed the biggest knife I could find and ran for the door and down the stairs.

When I reached the place where the conflict occurred, the enemies were retreating. I chased their truck on foot, and was gaining through the parking lot. Although quick on my toes, I failed to catch the perps. I'll never forget the look on the faces of the ones in the bed of the truck. I was running brandishing a large knife, and if they assumed I planned to use it, they assumed correctly.

An ambulance arrived, and soon I was strapped in and on my way to the hospital. I asked one of the paramedics on the way what he thought of my wound. He asked me how big the knife was. When I told him, he said that I should try to stay awake. I didn't think much of it. I focused on the overhead light. Before we reached the hospital, the light faded and I was in darkness.

They revived me at the hospital. I lost consciousness several times, and I remember having an out-of-body experience, seeing my own body in surgery. I remember leaving the surgery room and could see and hear my wife talking to a chaplain. He was informing her that I had passed and that the doctor was trying to revive me, he said I may not make it. He wanted to pray with her. Then there was darkness.

Again, I opened my eyes. I hadn't awakened in this world, but I woke in another. I was in my old neighborhood, the projects in East Dallas.

It was dark and the apartments were all boarded up. Gang graffiti was everywhere. The apartments had been run down when I lived there, with a lot of gang and drug activity. Apartments had been boarded up and graffiti covered some of the walls back then, but not like this. Now there were no people anywhere and I thought I must be in purgatory or even Hell.

A shadow moved in a nearby breezeway. I ran to make contact and when I entered the breezeway, no one was there. A barrel stood in the middle of the opening. I went to look inside the barrel and I remember feeling overwhelming grief. My wife was in the barrel. She was green. I turned the barrel on its side and pulled her out. I didn't understand what was happening. I cursed and yelled at God.

She disappeared and a light in the parking lot drew my attention. I walked out of the breezeway and considered the parking lot. There were no other lights on anywhere. The light that was on shone directly upon a small yellow car. I could see movement in the car. Two people fighting. I ran to the car and could see a man and woman inside. The woman was my wife and he was beating her.

I tried the door, but it was locked. I drew back and swung at the glass. I fell through the car and landed under the light. Then there was a voice, only a voice. It told me that I could live if I wanted and *It* would always be with me. *It* told me that I could have the chance to save my family, or I could let go. I chose to stay and when I woke in the hospital, my wife was sitting at the edge of my bed. I was tied down. The staff said I kept trying to fight. I remembered fighting. I remembered thinking how I should not have taken my eyes off the enemy. I had been in a coma for a week.

The Voice never left me. It's been one of the voices that guided me through many of my miseries. I wanted to be home for Christmas. The doctor said that if I used the bathroom on my own and walked every day, I could go home. I set my mind on recovery and *The Voice* urged me to move.

The hardest part was getting out of the bed. IVs and a stomach full of staples, like a zipper going right down my center, made it a challenge. I quit asking for apple juice and water. Every time I wanted a drink, *The Voice* chided me when I thought of using the call button. *It* reminded me of the goal and urged me to move again and again. My recovery progressed to the point that the nurses told me where they kept the juice and I'd get right into the cooler and get my own. I didn't tell anyone about the newly acquired *Voice*, *It* was my friend. *It* was a source of power, I felt stronger with *It*. It was as though God had given me a true friend. I wondered if *It* could be the voice of God at times.

I went home and my guardian guided me in many ways. *It* talked to me about what I was to do to succeed and warned me of dangers. I listened and rarely disputed what *It* said. *It* told me secrets about people and revealed to me their character. I had always been a decent judge of character, I thought. With *The Voice*, I began thinking differently.

At Christmas time, my family took plenty of pictures. My twin children were two years old and they tore into their presents. I was happy to be alive. Grateful to be with my family. When we developed the photos, there were oddities in the pictures of me. Grainy dots were in the photos I was in and I could see faces. I showed them to my wife and she could see what I saw, at least she said she could. I began to believe that I had something with me other than just *The Voice*. I wasn't sure at the time whether *It* was something good or evil.

I didn't want to do much on the streets until my stomach was healed. We were having financial issues since I couldn't hustle. *The Voice* told me I would come back better than ever, and I believed. *It* told me to be patient, and I was.

I woke one morning and saw what I thought to be smoke rolling on the floor. I woke my wife and got her and the children out of the house. I didn't see any fire in my apartment, so I started knocking on neighbors' doors. No one found fire in their apartments. I had people out of their homes early in the morning and there was no fire. I was embarrassed. I laid in my bed and saw the smoke again. I focused on it and realized it was a baby. An invisible see-through baby, crawling across the floor. I jumped out of the bed and opened my bathroom door, where it crawled into.

When I opened the door, I saw hundreds, maybe thousands of bright white dots swirling at eye level in the darkness. They swirled and came together. They began forming a being. A human-like figure, but badly distorted. I slammed the door and told my wife what I was seeing. She sympathized and we left the room to sit in the living room. I began seeing the see-through people everywhere.

They were in the kitchen, on the ceiling, the walls. I could make them out clearly. I saw them moving and watching me. In the hallway one stood; its shape changed constantly, but it was there. I thought they may be ghosts.

I wondered if they were coming from the nearby graveyard. I wondered if they were coming from people who'd died on the land. It was disturbing to the point that I was telling family and friends, trying to get them to my apartment and see if anyone else could see them. *The Voice* was telling me nothing I could use. *It* told me to stay calm. *It* warned me not to tell people. *It* said that they would judge me. They did. People laughed at me. They thought I was fried, asking me what kind of drugs I was on. I was completely sober. I had just woken from a good night's sleep.

I could see the 'ghosts' in the streets and on the

sidewalks. There were crowds of them. I wanted them to go away. Willing myself to ignore them did not work. On my own with this delusion, I was uncomfortable and acutely aware that I was going insane.

The people whom I had told about the visions would mention that day and say little sarcastic things about it. I never mentioned the see-through people anymore, I just accepted they were there and did my best to ignore them.

We received a letter shortly after the apparitions began. It said that we were being evicted for the 'gang fight' in the parking lot. I tried talking to the managers about it—they said I would have to appeal in writing. I decided instead to move to my mother's house. She lived alone and was happy to have my family and me there.

The intensity of my visions slowed almost to a halt. When I quit giving them as much power to disturb me, they quit being as predominant. They never went away entirely and I see them to this day. I have better coping skills than I had in the past and I do not let the spirits cause me to react today as I did when I first started noticing them. They are the worst in darkness. I always see them lurking in dark places.

The second pivotal moment

The second pivotal moment happened a few years later. I didn't speak to anyone about my visions, and had never spoke to anyone of *The Voice*, not even to my wife, to the best of my memory. I dealt with them silently. I was still guided by *The Voice* and had been doing well in my world. I'd acquired numerous vehicles and gained status in the streets. Progress came to a halt when my wife was arrested one evening.

I bailed her out of jail the next day and she told me the police officers who had arrested her had sexually assaulted her. I was furious. We went to the hospital and had tests done. Internal affairs officers belonging to the same police department came and took our story along with her clothing.

The follow up on the case was shoddy. They claimed to have tested the wrong officers for DNA and that they didn't have a good enough sample to run another test on the officers who actually arrested her. They said it was because she told them officer Williams raped her, when in actuality she had said that when she was being raped by one officer in the park, the other was saying, "Get her William. Get her William."

They claimed they tested officer Williams because of this. This officer Williams had been off duty at the time of the incident, and was probably a decent cop, while in fact, *William* was the *first name* of the man who was raping her. You would think that Internal Affairs detectives could figure this out without too much trouble, not that they would test the wrong man who wasn't even on duty at the time. You wouldn't think that Internal Affairs detectives wouldn't ignore the fact that she was arrested five minutes from the station and it took the arresting officers more than an hour from the arrest to walk her through the doors. You would think that her clothing, the physical evidence, wouldn't somehow be lost, but they were lost. The case became weak with the absence of physical evidence. It's odd to me how careless they were with the physical evidence. I must wonder how many alleged rape victim's clothes just happen to be lost on cases like this. How many times do you suppose they test the wrong subjects for DNA in what should have been a high-profile case? Why wouldn't they be able to put two and two together? These questions bother me to this day.

I'm not a police officer or investigator, although I do have an inquisitive mind and a thirst for knowledge and proclivity toward research. I have my opinions and I can see when things don't add up. How would she know the arresting officer's first name? They don't display that on their uniforms. They weren't friends and I can't imagine they were having a friendly conversation in the missing hour. As a matter of fact, a week or so before the arrest, my wife had gone to the store late one night with a friend, and when she returned, she said that a creepy officer had been staring at her and tried to talk to her outside of the store. My friend vouched for this, saying that the officer stared at them as they left the parking lot.

Almost immediately after the story of the creepy cop was told, he showed up at my house. He approached us (a group of friends, my wife and me) and his eyes kept wandering to her as he explained that he was there for a noise complaint. We were hooking up a stereo system in my Camaro out front. I knew it was a lie. We hadn't been making noise and we'd had the same neighbors since we bought the house. Our neighbors had never filed a noise complaint even during the wildest parties that we'd hosted almost every weekend. On this day, I hadn't even turned on the stereo I had been installing.

I can assume that, on the night he'd approached my wife in the store parking lot, he had run the license plate of the truck after they left the parking lot and found my address attached. I can assume that he was creeping on my wife. I can assume that he lied as an excuse of his presence. I can assume that, if there were a scouring of police records, there would be no record of the infamous call and the "noise complaint". I believe he began to plot against my wife that night.

On another night, at around one o'clock in the morning, I was walking home. He saw me and told me that if I didn't get in the car and let him take me home on my own, he would make me get in the car and find a reason to take me to the station. I got in the car. I told him I had been arguing with my wife and I was out walking to cool off. When we arrived, he let me out and told me not to do anymore arguing. My wife was sitting in the back of our truck, waiting. When he left, I told my wife that I had to go. I had been in a fight and I figured they might be back for me if they found out.

I ran up the street and heard tires screeching. I hid in some bushes and could see my wife. I watched the two cops come to a screeching halt behind my truck and get out to approach my wife. They started talking to her. It was the same two that arrested her on the night in question a week or so later. She told them that I had run off. I heard one of them yell at her, "You better not be fucking lying. If you are we'll get you, bitch!" I was furious, but what could I do?

Following another incident to do with paintball guns, we were stopped on the street. The officers making the stop were the same two cops with another, younger one. They listened to my explanation about an ongoing paintball war between some friends and me. Instead of arresting me, I was ticketed for a minor infraction. In the process of this traffic stop, they found out that my wife had warrants against her, as well as something in her purse, which gave them cause to take her in. I felt something funny when they drove away with her. I wanted to follow them, but the friend who was with me said I was tripping; he did not want to follow them to the police station. My wife made some disturbing calls home while in custody. Concerned, I checked the time on my ticket compared to the time she was brought in, and noticed over an hour's gap. There were approximately three traffic lights and only a mile or so distance between the location where she was arrested and the police station.

Following her arrest, release and the subsequent filing of a report on the officers for rape, my wife wouldn't sleep. She would stand in the window of my childhood home and cry. She told me they were going to come for us. She said they'd warned her that if she told anyone, they would lock me up and kill her. You can imagine what this did to supercharge my psychological disorders. I was going crazy inside. We started staying in hotels and my mother didn't feel comfortable anymore in the house we had called home for more than a decade. We all left and I lived like I was on the run. From city to city and in and out of hotels.

At the hotels, I began hearing more than the one voice in my mind, then something new happened. I began having auditory hallucinations to the extreme. I started hearing screaming in the middle of the night, like someone was being tortured. I could hear it coming through the walls and sometimes I thought children were being held and mistreated. I would wake my wife and make her listen. If a friend was there, I would have them listen. They all said I was going crazy. I quit reaching out for help and my sickness became worse as time went on. My wife and friends could see it, but they didn't know what was going on with me.

We stayed at one hotel for a long period. We rented it by the week. Sometimes my wife and I would go to Dallas. We had two trucks, and one wasn't registered in my name. I preferred to drive the one that wasn't in my name in case the local police pulled behind me. The officers involved in our case were supposed to be on leave per our attorney. This was information he'd said he had acquired from the police department.

One night, returning to the hotel late, all the parking spaces were taken. I pulled behind the truck that was in my name and could see a man in a 90's model blue Chevy step side pickup directly across from mine. He was pulled in backwards and we made eye contact. It was the officer who had arrested my wife that night, William. He was in his police uniform, but in what looked like a personal vehicle.

I drove past and he began following me. I called a close family friend and he told me he was too far away to help. He said to call 911 and tell them what was happening. I did. I dialed 911 and told the operator that an officer accused of assaulting my wife was following me in a personal vehicle, in uniform, and that he was supposed to be on suspension. I told them that he must be off his rocker and planning to do something to us. She told me to stay on the phone. I entered the highway. I could see a police cruiser with his cherries on entering the next ramp onto the highway, he was behind us shortly.

The cruiser didn't get behind him, it got behind me. I knew this must be a friend of the rogue cop. The 911 operator told me that she'd just been informed that the officers were investigating and just wanted to ask me some questions. I explained to her that I didn't believe they had questions for me. I told her I didn't want to pull over until there were more cruisers, a supervisor.

A second patrol car came and I exited the highway. The dispatcher told me if I kept going I could get an evading charge. I told her to be sure to send more police. I pulled over, and soon an officer approached. I couldn't see the officer who was approaching with the lights in my mirror. When I tried to speak as he walked up, he told me, "Shut the fuck up."

It was the other officer from the night they told my wife they would get her and from the night of her arrest in question. There were two other officers there, besides the two from the night of the arrest. The one that was there the night of my wife's arrest was riding in his own patrol car and the two I hadn't seen before were riding together and the other from the arrest was in the blue pickup.

The two from the night of the arrest started walking me down into a valley beside the road. The other two got my wife out of the truck. I could hear her telling them she wanted to make a call. I looked back and they were crowding her by the passenger side view mirror. She was holding our cell phone. One of those officers barked, "You better not touch that phone, bitch! I'll fucking smash it." She was crying and the other one started yelling at her to shut the fuck up.

The officers in question told me to get down on one knee, in the valley. The one named William paced in front of me with a side arm that didn't look like police issue. It was chrome, and my memory says it was a revolver. I'm not naïve enough to think anything less than malicious intent. I asked, "What the fuck are you doing here?"

He said, "I'm looking for bad guys."

I told him he should go home and look in the mirror. The officer behind me, holding my arms above my head at the wrist said, "Do it." to someone I could hear walking up in the grass.

I laughed. I told him, "Go ahead, do it. More of your friends will be here soon. I just got off the phone with them."

He stared into my eyes and I know he could see that I wasn't lying or scared in that moment. Within seconds of our interaction, police cruisers started showing up in multiples. The newly arriving troves of officers went to my wife and also came down into the valley with me. One of the officers told the two in question to get off the scene. They grouped my wife and me behind my truck. The head officer told us that it was all a fluke. He said if they had known it was us in the truck they would not have approached us. He said they were on a detail, searching for car thieves in the area we were in.

Isn't it a hell of a coincidence that I had no adult record at that date, but as a juvenile I had several unauthorized use of a motor vehicle charges? Isn't it a greater coincidence the officer accused of assaulting my wife had been in an unmarked vehicle, parked behind a truck that was in my name? Is it coincidence—merely a fluke—that he looked me in the eyes before chasing me? Am I supposed to believe they didn't realize it was my wife and I when they walked me into a valley and put me in a questionable position? When the other officers were threatening to smash our cell phone out of my wife's hands? Was that justified? Do these sound like the actions of innocent men? Not to me. The mental instabilities caused by stress, aggravation and paranoia after this incident were crippling.

Our attorney tried to get the 911 recordings as evidence for our case, but he said the police refused to give him the recordings and refused to cooperate with him on the case. Anxiety and frustration grew inside of me and the voices would not quiet. I thought I was being stalked and followed so much that I quit talking to a lot of the people I knew. We decided we had to get away from the city for a while and went to stay with a friend in East Texas. I suffered severely from hallucinations and became too sick to deal with people. I could hear voices and see horrible things. Visions of murder and rape clouded my mind.

We secured our own place and stayed on thirty acres of land in a little house. There were no neighbors in the back of us, but the voices would tell me there were people in the woods. At night, I would stare out of the window with a shotgun in my hands. I could see them in the trees. To me they were there, crouching and watching us in the darkness. I started hearing screams and cries for help. I would go outside and hear a baby crying somewhere in the woods. I would hear men laughing. I didn't want to shoot. I didn't know if there were innocent people or a baby out there. I began exercising excessively to take my mind off the voices, laughter and screams.

I wasn't making any money, so eventually we had to move back to the city to live once again with my mother. I lived in the loft of my mother's apartment, with my wife. I began to think that things were happening all the time that my wife didn't want to tell me about. I attempted to put cameras everywhere to catch somebody doing something to her. I began thinking that whoever it was doing these things knew how to make themselves invisible and could disappear in a blink of the eyes. *I could see them, though.* The more I concentrated, the more I could see them. I tried to make out who they were. The severity of my delusions escalated to the point that I would record white noise and watch it. I thought I could see what was happening in the white and black dots. I could see figures and hear the noises. Screams of pain or moans of pleasure.

We moved from the apartment. My wife and I separated. I was so disturbed in my thoughts that I was afraid I might hurt her. I thought it best for us to be apart. I didn't want to hurt her. I got rid of all my weapons and went to live with a friend. I had begun to be physically ill. I thought I was dying. I went to the hospital several times, and each time I thought the personnel were lying when they said they couldn't find anything physically wrong. I believed that people were poisoning me, so I wouldn't eat anything others prepared for me.

I didn't leave my room often. I didn't communicate like I used to. People would reach out to me and I was ashamed of the things that went through my head, so I wouldn't tell them what was happening. *The Voice* itself had developed what I would equate to Tourette's syndrome. It cursed so loudly when people talked to me that I couldn't concentrate. My paranoias grew from believing that the police were stalking me to thinking that average people were helping them.

My wife and I reconciled for a time, but I was mentally far gone. Friends would visit me, but I wasn't the same person they remembered. I had been a much-loved family man, but now I began to feel ostracized. I became agitated and violent. I used to preach love, but now my hatred for the police and my perceived enemies began to ooze through so that my mind constantly churned with hatred. It's a terrible thing what happens to a man when sanity is slipping.

Nightmares ate me alive, sleeping and awake. I became violent, so my wife asked me to leave. I didn't argue. I knew I had deteriorated mentally so that I was basically no good to anyone. I began roaming the streets constantly with nowhere to go. I turned to drugs to stay awake and keep the nightmares at bay. My hallucinations increased and I was lost. No one could communicate with me successfully in that state of mind. I became quiet and was so sick and numb I would rarely react or make facial expressions when people talked to me.

The third pivotal moment

My brother-in-law, William Necessary, was watching fireworks on 4th of July that year with my pregnant sister. He stepped out of the car and was run over by a drunken driver. The guy drove a distance with William on the front clip of the car. Smashing his breaks, he threw Will off the hood into a ditch and sped away as though Will meant nothing.

Friends and family had to search to find my brother in the darkness of the ditch, where he had been discarded to die. Paramedics took Will to the hospital in critical condition. He died a few days later in a hospital bed with his body full of tubes.

My sister was left to give birth to Will's second child in loneliness and loss. Will had been preparing to join the army. He had big dreams of designing video games. My fondest memories of Will are the times we stayed up all night taking turns with the controller to beat video games together.

His son is one of my favorite people in the world and, often, I can see his father in him. It hurts me that he never got the chance to meet his dad. I wish I'd had more time with Will. I am happy that my sister eventually found someone who accepts her and my nephew as his own. I know my sister still hurts for Will. Anyone who would have known him would miss him today.

I was in shock from Will's death to the extent that I didn't want to see him with all the tubes in him. When I heard that he wasn't going to make it I had to leave the hospital before they pulled the life support. Alone, I smashed the gas on my truck and cursed the heavens. The mental stresses this added to me were extreme. The last conversation Will and I had hadn't been a good one and now I can only tell him how much he meant to me to the wind, hoping that he might be able to hear me.

The fourth pivotal moment

During my ongoing dilemma, my other brother-in-law, Derrick Smith, was killed by police almost six months to the day of Will's death, on New Year's Eve. They said he was reaching for a gun when they responded to a call at his parents' household. I was told the gun was behind the couch and unloaded. That would be suicide by police and I didn't believe he would do that. My last memory—or at least the one that lives in my head—the memory that I cherish of Derrick, was when I got an S/10 blazer and brought it for him to see. He liked the burnt orange paint job with gold flakes and gold spoke rims. I can never forget his reaction when I pulled out the switch box for the hydraulics.

I started hitting the switches and he lit up. It brings tears to my eyes. I wish so badly that I would have handed the keys and title to him. I used to do things like that before I became so ill that I lost everything. Seeing him so excited—I remember thinking about it all the way home. It kills me inside that I didn't attend the funeral. I can't forgive myself for being so messed up in the head that I wasn't there for my step-sister and Derrick.

I love all my brothers. William and Derrick will always be missed and loved. R.I.P.—I wish you were here.

There were numerous deaths through my sickness. Some of them were because of the sickness in the individuals and some were due to other tragic turns of fate. The deaths of my family and friends haunt me and I know they are still with me in spirit.

The conclusion of my wife's case

The police department turned on my wife. They dismissed the case on the officers and charged her with filing a false police report. Through the last leg of the battle she didn't tell me what was happening, because we were separated by that time. I knew she wanted to give up on the fight against the officers during our separation. I told her that everything would come to light when the case made it to trial.

I had an open case I was waiting on trial for. When I got my jury trial, I was found not guilty. My wife and I had the same lawyer. He shook my hand and told me, "That takes care of you both."

I asked him what he meant and he told me that my wife had signed for probation. Probation—she had pled guilty to the false report charge! I was sick. I wanted to punch him in the face right there in the court room. I left the building and my wife picked me up with a friend. I didn't want to bring it up in front of anyone. It was too emotional.

We drove straight to my friend's place and my friend asked me to come to the garage. Another one of my friends was there. He had a bottle of liquor and they wanted to celebrate my win. I wanted to tell them what the lawyer told me, but I couldn't bring myself to do it. I shed tears and left the house without a word. My morale was crushed.

That's when I began driving, constantly. It seemed like when I drove, I could ease the pressure on my brain. I wanted to explode. The voices taunted me. My insides boiled. I became more introverted. I was alert about police and didn't pull over and submit to arrest willingly in my home town. I figured the officers hadn't dropped their grudge, because I couldn't find it in myself to be at peace in any measure.

When flagged by police, I abandoned my vehicle and ran, leaving the vehicle to be impounded and ultimately lost. That scenario was repeated until I'd lost every vehicle I owned. I couldn't find peace. The anger in me toward the police and the world afforded me no comfort. There was little pleasure in anything.

The fifth pivotal moment

I was at a friend's home late one night getting ready to go out of town. When I got ready to leave, he asked if I would take him to get a hamburger. We drove to the closest all night joint. After getting our food, we headed back toward his home. We took back roads and got lit up by police at a stop sign close to my in-laws' home in Grand Prairie.

I sped to their house and jumped out, running around the house into the backyard. I jumped the fence and ran down the alley. I hid in someone's shed until morning, curled up like a dog in a tiny space between garden tools. I decided to walk out of the city before calling anyone, so that's what I did. When I got to the city of Irving, I walked to a friend's house and asked for a ride. *The Voice* guided me the whole way, my best friend.

I had a car parked in Arlington and I had to hot wire it since I had lost my keys. I wanted to go to my father's home in the country, like I had planned, but I didn't have gas. A friend called me and said he didn't have anywhere to go with his girl. They had money and I needed gas. I figured we could ride out to my father's place and relax a while.

I got to my dad's that night and everybody was asleep. I remember I couldn't sleep and I let my friends lay down in my bedroom. My wife had been staying out there and she showed up in the morning and caused a ruckus when she found my friends in the bed. My father woke up and my wife and I were going at it. My father told me I had to leave.

I went back to the city and a friend told me they found the guy who had been in the car with me when

I ran—they'd found him dead in his house. I didn't know what to think of it. When I found out I was a suspect, I really didn't know what to think. The police were looking for me for questioning, but I felt I was being set up. *The Voice* told me that they were going to pin it on me. I agreed. In my mind, the officers we had gone up against in the assault case gone bad were likely behind it. After everything I'd been through, the stress kept building and my mental state was severely warped.

Not knowing where to go, I started staying below the radar. Basically, I had to live completely illegal if I was going to stay free. I was alienated from any type of normal life and mentally sick. The places you stay in a situation like this are high risk environments.

I ran for many months and my mentality deteriorated rapidly. Within months, I began staring into space for long periods of time. I was constantly exposed to things that only further induced hallucinations. Those months when I was running were some of the worst in my life.

Being in the mindset that I had to be in, and as sick as I was, my situation and circumstances became overwhelming. Over those months, I ran repeatedly from police and when they finally caught me, I had multiple evading arrest charges backlogged against me. They didn't even ask me about the man who was killed when I was booked in. Apparently, they'd found the murderer days before they found me. I only overheard that they had caught the murderer and never inquired about details. I was happy it was over, but my sickness had developed in such a way that it would be years before I was stable.

I want to go into detail about the types of

hallucinations I experienced over the years. They began with *The Voice*. I call the voice '*It*'. *It* has always stayed with me. The progression of the disease worsened rapidly over the years. Counseling and medication help me to be productive today.

Even after I was released from jail for all the evading arrest charges, I had nowhere to stay. My family didn't want me there and my wife had begun a relationship with someone else. I was on my own in the streets and staying wherever I could. Hell wasn't done with me yet.

In the years that followed, eventually, I began to be admitted to hospitals by family and friends. I'm grateful for the times they tried to help. I know they didn't understand what was going on with me because I didn't talk about it. That's no one's fault but mine.

5 MY HALLUCINATIONS

In this section I will go into detail about the types of hallucinations I experienced and how they affected me. Keep in mind that these accounts are not necessarily in chronological order, because many of these hallucinations happened simultaneously. All the hallucinations were and are reoccurring. They tortured and haunted me for many years without relief—without medication. I experience the same types of hallucinations now as I did over the years of progression on occasion. I'm very fortunate to have people in my life today that care enough about me and my health to help me stay somewhat sane—Doctors, probation officer, counselors, family and friends. My support network is a must.

Bugs in my skin

I first began examining myself too closely early in my disease. I thought tiny bugs were burying themselves in my skin. I would look at my cuticles and think I could see their heads sticking out. I searched up and down my arms and legs with a magnifying glass and tried to get other people to see the imaginary bugs. I would get in the shower and rub parts of my skin raw.

During this phase of the sickness I believed that my body was riddled with menacing creatures. I rarely dug into my skin trying to get them out, but it was a predominant thought and temptation to do so. Eventually, other problems became so great that the bug problem didn't register as an immediate threat, so I would ignore the bugs. No one ever saw them in my skin. This kind of hallucination can cause various complications. You begin to wonder where the bugs are coming from and inspecting surfaces, food and drinks, your stool. You worry about bedding, clothing and the ground.

Paranoia about being poisoned

I developed paranoias about being poisoned. I wouldn't eat food that anyone prepared for me. I thought family, friends and acquaintances were trying to get rid of me. My sickness told me that they didn't want me around. Sometimes I would eat to get it over with and I lived. The voices told me that no one wanted me to live. They told me I was worthless and causing problems for everyone when I showed up.

I came to a place in my mind where I would only risk drinking from water hoses and faucets in front of random people's homes. I found a pear tree and would go there often to eat. Looking back, I didn't know if they used pesticides on the fruit and I would eat it without washing it, sometimes. If I were to be poisoned anywhere that would be a most likely place; nonetheless, I listened to the voices and believed that people in my life were purposely trying to poison me. Sometimes, I wouldn't eat for days, maybe even weeks, until I was hospitalized. Even then, I would be hesitant because of the next delusion/hallucination. This type of hallucination makes you untrusting of the people you should be able to trust. It stems from thinking you're unwanted. The delusion will cause you to act very much differently with people than you normally would. When people ask what's wrong, you usually don't trust them enough to tell them. The distrust builds and may erupt into aggression. Hallucinations like this are some of the worst, in my opinion.

Believing that food was actually human flesh

The voices would tell me that the food people were trying to serve me was human. They told me the appearance of the food was an illusion. The voices told me that the people made it look like regular food, but it was human. I resisted eating or lost my appetite on multiple occasions. No food was safe. At this time, the voices and hallucinations revolved around war, something I will go into further detail about later. Basically, *The Voice* convinced me that the war had halted the delivery of most food and that they were serving my enemies' bodies disguised as normal foods, like eggs or grapes. *The Voice* might tell me an omelet was made of a human hand, or that a grape was actually an eyeball, or that a pear halve was a tongue.

This went on for so long that when I finally began eating the foods after being hospitalized, I felt remorse. I thought that maybe the voices were testing me and that I had failed when I consumed. I remember thinking that I was eating body parts, yet I didn't stop eating. I wasn't sure what that said about me as a person. I guess I could have starved myself longer. I doubt the voices would have let up before I either died or found myself being fed through a tube.

This hallucination had the effect of alienating me from the ones I loved. I didn't want to go around them, because I didn't want to be made to eat them. I tried to tell myself that this was a delusion, but the voices and hallucinations were persistent and very much real to me.

Aliens

I believed that I had become some sort of a project to alien creatures. I thought they could shape-shift and turn into people I knew or encountered. It was extremely disturbing to think that everyone I had ever known was now a possibly malevolent being. They could change fast. I would believe that my people were being put into different bodies and made to stop communicating with me. I saw eyes of others and recognized them, only to be let down while wandering the earth essentially lost.

This hallucination happened on and off for years and still disturbs me. It's hard for me to believe that it was all delusion, even heavily medicated I remember how real these things were to me. I could see people I knew in the glimmer of a stranger's eyes. I could hear familiar voices from friends and family, but if I tried to communicate they would leave. The aliens, like other hallucinations, could change in a blink of the eyes. This anomaly lasted for what seemed like an eternity.

The alien-body-shifter hallucination had the effect on my mentality to distrust that people were who they said they were. I would accuse people I knew of being someone they weren't, or I would simply ignore them, not saying anything at all. On the other side of that coin, I would want to be around people I barely knew, because I thought they were possessed with the people I did know and trust. It was a harmful delusion. It also served to alienate me from those whom may have helped me.

I wandered the streets for days and weeks searching for someone I knew. All my effort to make contact failed, and even when I was around people I knew, I thought they were strangers, posing. Imagine how this might feel and how you could cope with this delusion. I had no tools to deal with this. Insane and alone is where this hallucination led me.

Messages through radios and televisions

When I miss doses of medication, one of the first delusions usually has to do with the radio and television. This is always a catch 22. When I begin to become delusional, I don't like the quiet. When it's quiet, the voices torment me. They start having disturbing conversations in my mind and I begin to argue; in turn, my stress levels rise and cause more problems.

I turn the radio or television on to try to drown out the noise. Preferably the radio, because I think that, unlike the television, a radio might not be able to watch me. The radio will say things that I think are directly linked to what I'm thinking or doing. The television is worse. I'm convinced the television can see me. There weren't many days I could watch a program and not think I'm somehow intertwined in the dialog of it, even if I've seen the exact show before. I have this delusion some days at present, even with medication.

When I'm hallucinating, I think that the television is alive and everything that happens there is for a purpose to gain a reaction from me, to disturb me. I am unable to get comfortable and enjoy a show. I eventually pace around and until I get medication and sleep it doesn't stop being overwhelming and disturbing.

One of the drawbacks to this delusion is that I became distant to the world and everything happening in it. Most people enjoy watching television. I would go to family or friend's homes and get extremely disturbed by the television. It would cause what I call 'bad vibes'. I would be asked to leave on most occasions. It resulted in hospitalization sometimes. Other times I would just be dropped off on some street corner or at a drug house.

Power to raise spirits to roam the earth

I was living in a house with no water and wallowing in poverty, insanity and filth. I went to the garage and found some things. There was a circular plastic container with chambers. I filled a chamber with soda, another with cheese crackers and another with dirt. I made a bridge from one chamber to the next with wood and strings. Then I put an electric candle that flickered like a flame, an Indian statue and another relic in a triangle around the container.

I believed that a society would grow in the container. I left it overnight. When I came back, I believed I could see little people walking across my bridges. They were like the other transparent people I would see, but small. *The Voice* told me that I had summoned the Mayans and that they would become great warriors for me.

This only served to further my descent into insanity. The Mayans grew and along with them came the words, "We eat what we kill."—a disturbing thought that would bring me to horrible places in my mind and gave me visions full of running, screaming people, apparently, hallucinations. At the time, they were as real to me as anything else. I didn't know how to return the Mayans to wherever I'd brought them from and they multiplied with the years. I didn't speak of them to anyone that I remember.

This hallucination made me feel pleasure at first. I liked having a bigger army. They spoke a foreign language to me, but I understood it somehow. The more they grew and multiplied, the more chaos they brought to me. Eventually, I was able to banish them. I haven't had this hallucination in many years, but I know that the Mayans could return. I know that without medication and education, this delusion's return is possible.

Having this delusion was especially disturbing because I felt I had brought it upon myself. In some ways, I had, but that's the thing about being sick—for some reason, we do things that serve to make us sicker. Although I had performed a ritual so that what happened with the Mayans essentially formed within my mind through a deliberate task, it was one of the more violent and vile delusions I manifested and I didn't realize exactly what I was doing when I did it.

For almost everything I've experienced, I have concluded that most of my delusions and discomforts were formed in some way by my own sickness. The catalysts from earlier circumstances somehow kick-started a greater sickness that was always within me. The Mayans and the types of rituals I performed throughout my sickness, along with my superstitions, fed my disease.

The mirrors are watching

I couldn't bring myself to look in the mirror often. *It* was there. *The Voice*, he was in the mirror and the mirror was the only place I could truly see him. I didn't like to look in the mirror when *It* was angry, or if there were other people in the room. I didn't know what *It* would do to someone in the room with me looking in the mirror. *It* did tell me *It* would take their eyes. I believed this, because *It* was always with me. At times, *it* showed me what *It* would do. At a glance in the mirror, whoever was in the room with me would be missing their eyes. I had to look directly at them, face to face, to give them their eyes back. *It* warned me about the mirror. I knew I shouldn't look in the mirror unless I was alone—and sometimes, not even then.

The mirror was alive. *It* could watch me closely in a mirror. *It* liked that I didn't want to see *it*. *It* became a destroyer and capable of anything. Whenever I went near a mirror, I could see *It* watching me in the corner of my eye, facing me and daring me to look. *It* was smart and *It* was always there. I went a long time without looking directly in the mirror.

This hallucination made it hard for me to keep up with my appearance. Most of the time, I had no idea what I looked like. So much time would pass without me looking directly into a reflective surface, that when I did, it wasn't unusual for me to see a completely different person. I tried to wait until I was alone to look into a mirror, but I could always see *It* in my eyes. Being easy to agitate *It*, I didn't spend much time at the mirror or looking directly into the reflection of my own eyes. What lived there was something unpleasant, a violent warrior. He was mad when we weren't winning.

Ubiquitous cameras and microphones

There were times I believed anything could be a microphone or camera. It started when I would tape up all the holes and cracks in the walls, ceiling fans, smoke detectors, etc. I thought people were watching me from somewhere because the voices would tell me things I was about to do or the television or radio seemed to know everything I was doing. The situation was hopeless. No matter what I did, I felt the eyes of the world were on me. *It* told me that anything could be a camera or microphone. *It* told me there was no use trying to stop the world from seeing me.

Paranoia ate at my core. It didn't matter where I was, inside or outside, the world would watch. I could hear their voices and jokes. They laughed at me. They enjoyed my struggle. *It* would battle the world that hated me. That's what *It* told me. *It* said that the world loved my pain and suffering. *It* wanted to show the world pain and suffering. *It* told me to let them watch all they wanted. *It* said people are most curious of what they know little about. *It* said I was different and that's why they watched and enjoyed my suffering.

This hallucination made me paranoid about everything I did. I didn't think I could use the bathroom without someone watching. I felt bitter about the laughter. I was angry that I struggled and no one would help. I despised the jokes and the looks. This delusion helped me become withdrawn from the world.

When you think the world is laughing at you, watching and enjoying your misery, you become despondent and desensitized to the world around you. The delusion that 'everyone is against you' makes the hallucinations bearable to some degree, in the sense that you begin to think most people are your enemies. The army that *It* was commanding for me was against my enemies. I didn't like it when we fell behind, either.

The suffering of this delusion made me think I was surrounded at times, and the chaos that ensued throughout my days was like being suspended in a world of madness and treachery. I look back on these days and it was real to me. I don't understand how these things could have been as real and intense and only been in my head. I do know that today, with my coping skills and focus on positivity, it's hard for me to believe I experienced all this and yet have found my way to a better place—one where I see the world and welcome it, where I'm not overly concerned about being watched or laughed at.

Finding myself in the fires of Hell

I could feel the flames burning my body. *It* told me that I was the Devil. It said that I've visited Hell since the beginning of its existence. *It* claimed to be the eighth most powerful spirit in the world. Although it was the eighth most powerful spirit in world, it was *the* most powerful spirit in Hell. *It* said that all spirits more powerful than *It* were in another realm, and they cared not what happened in ours because we were the damned, yet we were at the top of the chain of command in Hell. *It* began calling me Lucifer. *It* told me my armies were gathering and that all my enemies were going to suffer.

I began to be unconcerned whether people liked me. I trusted that *It* knew who my enemies were in the spirit realm and otherwise. I believed *It* could see them and deal with them more freely than I could. It didn't matter to me that I had no place in the world and that nobody seemed to care for me. There's no sympathy for the Devil, and I didn't expect any. I became immersed in a world of chaos. I became a shape-shifter and there was no place truly for me.

This delusion lasted the better part of a decade. I was at war, my mind and eardrums filled with what *It* told me were the screams of my enemies. I didn't react to these things anymore. *It* did all the work and I only had my consciousness that never ceased to bring me to new heights of depravity. Some things that I saw in this state of mind I'd rather not speak of. They were transparent visions, sickening and disturbing. I was tortured the same as my enemies. Eventually, those who I cared for haunted my visions and I believed that the world I lived in was a wasteland.

I believed myself a Christian all my life, but the love wasted out of me leaving me empty inside. I was told I was the Devil—I rebuked this, but believed it. The times I had to seize up during these hallucinations are so numerous I can't remember them all. *It* would tell me to freeze and I froze. *It* was in me and I was Lucifer. *It* protected me from my enemies. Although I don't believe I'm the Devil today, I don't know that this hallucination would be avoidable if I ran out of medication for a week or longer. I visit other 'worlds' in my mind; being the Devil in Hell was only one of the many.

This hallucination made me question the reality of anything and everything around me. Living out this delusion made me uncomfortable in church and around people who talked about God. All my life I had believed in God. These were some of the darkest days. I felt abandoned by God and the world. My mind was filled with conflict and confusion.

Coming out of this delusion was no easy task. I don't think I could have escaped it on my own. In the end, it was the love of others that brought me back. Being in Hell wasn't a delusion that made me healthy in any way. The levels of insanity and sickness this hallucination brought me are powerful and unyielding. I still remember so much of it and I don't like to think of it. I'm grateful that I have survived and surpassed this delusion.

My invisible army

There was always an army with me. I was a General. *The Voice* was there as always. Gunshots would ring out, throughout the day and night. I would watch the army of transparent beings pile the bodies at my feet. They, too, were transparent. I could see their clothing, but could see through them. Guns littered the floor. When it was time to move, my soldiers would attach body armor to me, and *It* would guide me to the next location.

The world was a war zone in my mind and everything was falling apart. I wasn't sure I would make it back from these delusions. I walked from city to city with squads of heavily armed soldiers at my sides, front and back, destroying anything that stood in the way or tried to stop us.

I would rest under highway overpasses. I watched the cars until *The Voice* told me that it was time to move again. The invisible army protected me, and at times, when I fell in enemy hands, I would be told by *It* to shut down. They came for me. They always came for me. I couldn't explain this to anyone. We were at war. If I acknowledged these things, I thought *It* would leave me. I didn't want *It* to leave me. *The Voice* was my friend. *It* was my warrior. *It* was all I had to keep me company in the madness.

I would hear *It* knocking down doors to get to me. *It* never stopped. *It* didn't believe in surrender. The soldiers had flack and heavy machine guns. There were tanks and helicopters at our disposal. The capabilities of my army were endless in my mind. They were a predominant delusion. *It* would not let me be taken for long or die in enemy hands. *It* always knew where I was because we were connected. *It* was, and still is, part of me.

This hallucination could be disturbing at times, but mostly it entertained me. There's a level of separation involved in this delusion. A hallucination like this can keep a person distant from the world, while the visions it produces are lasting and graphic.

I believe the hallucination derived out of necessity. My mind made it so I didn't have to fight alone. God gave me the army as I am sure he gives me consciousness and all other things. Even the Devil is owned by God, because God is the ultimate Creator. It's how I organized His gifts that became disturbing. Although disturbing, the curse is a gift that I will go into greater detail about further in this book.

Nano-bots

I HAD BEEN INJECTED WITH TINY ROBOTS. The robots gave me radio wave communication capabilities and could do useful things, like provide a force shield. The robots bordered on being mind-controllers, but ultimately, I was in control. I began hearing more voices and I believed the Nano-bots made it so that some unknown humans, the watchers, could follow me.

The Nano-bots were the reason that the television and radio spoke to me, I thought. The Nano-bots could also increase my strength and stamina. They were unfamiliar—a whole separate entity than *It*. I could get transmissions from the Nano-bots about others, I thought.

The voices were numerous, because the frequency made it so that I could hear whoever was controlling the bots clearly. They tried to get me to submit to their deeds through the Nano-bots. After I gave strong resistance, they fried the bots and I pissed them out. They were very slick about it. They didn't tell me, but I believed I knew. This delusion went on for a long period. I always tried to convince myself that it was a delusion. *It* took precautionary measures against the bots and told me *It* was creating static, to block their signal at times. I didn't like this delusion, because it made me uncertain about myself. I didn't know exactly who the watchers were, or what they wanted.

Not knowing who might be trying to control you, or what their intentions might be, breeds paranoia. It's irrational and random, some might think. On the contrary, as I've said before, with a progressive mental disorder these things are very real. They are so real that you wonder why it is that 'they' would go through so much effort just to watch you suffer—whoever 'they' were.

Maybe 'they' were no one. I can believe that the Nano-bots were a delusion, but it's a hard one to discard sometimes. I'm not sure exactly what the purpose of this delusion was. What I do know is that I am relieved to not be suffering it at the time of this writing.

Others can read my mind

After my brain started to become clouded by so many voices I could hardly think, something happened. I did begin thinking, and the numerous voices would answer. Just think about how much trash our heads are filled with—the thought of anyone hearing your thoughts would be disturbing, right? It was for me. I began to believe that the world could hear my thoughts. I hated it.

Have you ever tried to stop thinking? How about when voices are in your head saying disturbing things? I have voices in my head, and I've been in many silent conflicts. There have also been times where my thoughts alone caused conflicts. I talk to *It* all the time, but many new voices came as well. Women, children, friends, family, strangers—I could hear them all in my head. I wanted to die there were so many voices.

I couldn't rest; they were always there saying awful things or just nonsense. This was different than the previous audible hallucinations I'd experienced. Although the audible hallucinations were disturbing, it was rare that I believed they could hear my thoughts until this started happening. I still have conflict with the voices, but these days I throw most of what they say overboard.

Movies on the walls

I began seeing scenes on the walls and other surfaces like car head rests, floors and almost any other flat surface. I would watch these transparent scenes for hours sometimes. It would show me faces and violent interactions, people having sex, all types of deranged things. If I tried to shut my eyes and not see the visions, I could see them on the backs of my eyelids. Another crafty way my sickness tortured me.

There was nonstop action. Rest wasn't an option. I could only sleep after severe exhaustion. When I did sleep, the visions didn't stop. Often I would wake and the visions would be worse than before I had rest. With medication and proper rest, it's better. I still have intense nightmares; they just don't seem as real.

If you can imagine the context of this hallucination and the types of things I thought about and experienced, you may begin to understand how unsettling these experiences were to me. There were masked figures walking through rooms. Murder, rape and war. Having these things plague me in so many ways made me hesitant to trust anyone or anything.

My eyes are cameras

I thought I was in a movie. I thought the world was watching everything I was doing. *The Voice* told me my eyes were cameras. I believed *It* because everyone's eyes are cameras. They feed visual information to the brain to be processed. The voices made me believe that I was director and main attraction. I would watch everything like a show. I believed some strange things about this. Something I call the 'eye game'.

I didn't want to tell anyone about this hallucination because *It* said 'they' would want to take my eyes. Sometimes I felt pressure in my eyes as though someone were trying to pull them out. I like my eyes as much as anyone else might like theirs. I didn't want to talk about this delusion with anyone, because I wanted to keep my vision.

The eye game

The Voice told me that moving my eyes to the left

would fast forward. To the right everything would rewind. If I looked down, everything was supposed to stop. *It* said I couldn't force this. *It* said my movements had to be natural. I believed I was screwing the world up with the eye game. I was the remote, with no control.

I didn't like this hallucination at all. There was one time that the world paused around me when I was in a store. I turned my head from left to right and everyone was frozen. I had experienced similar things, but the phenomena had only lasted split seconds before. This time, it happened and I looked at the people and out the window at the cars. Everything was paused. I don't understand this hallucination. I don't know how it's possible, but it happened.

Everything paused but me. How could this happen? I have thought about it for years and I just don't know. Sometimes I think that this delusion was orchestrated. I think the world knew I was sick and they were messing with me. You might call it paranoia, or try to explain it away, but it's a difficult one for me because the world paused and I can't explain it. This hallucination seemed one of the most real and the world seemed to be in on it.

Thinking people were messing with me made me more of an introvert. I didn't trust anyone. You can imagine my concern when no one popped out and said, "Gotcha!" It was hard for me to understand what anyone was getting out of it if it were in fact real. I must think that these things were merely a hallucination today, but it's difficult to write off, being one of the weirdest things that happened to me.

Screams from other rooms

A severely disturbing delusion would be the

JOHN U. GUNTER

screams from family and friends in the other rooms of whatever home I would be in. I would be sitting by myself in the next room and hear screams like one of them was getting tortured or attacked. I'd run into the next room ready for action. You can imagine how I startled everyone.

It became so aggressive and difficult, I paced and stormed around the house until I began to sweat, or I sat and listened to the screams without budging, because I thought there was nothing I could do but make it worse. Keep in mind that these were audible hallucinations. I could hear them like something was happening that I could do nothing about. There were multiple voices taunting me. They would tell me to come outside and face them and they would leave my family alone. I would go outside and there was no one there to fight.

They would tell me to come into the garage or the next room, so they could kill me. They said if I let them kill me they would leave the people I cared about alone. All lies. They were never outside or in the next room, or the garage. The screams would persist. There were the transparent people and taunting voices, but they wouldn't give me rest. There was no release. I was being tortured to the extreme.

This hallucination was one of the most frequent. The delusions wouldn't stop whether I slept, changed locations or tried to ignore them. The voices and transparent people persisted. These hallucinations caused my family to drop me off at hospitals and caused me to go insane in silence.

Imagine hearing screams from those you care for and not being able to do anything about it, no matter how hard you tried. Think of what this type of delusion would do to you. What if the voices told you not to tell anyone what you were experiencing or they would make it real? They would torture and kill your family. Would you tell anyone enthusiastically? I didn't.

As a matter of fact, these hallucinations were the ones that kept me silent the longest. I told myself the screams weren't real, but they were very real to me. Real enough for me to stalk in agitation through the homes of my loved ones until I was ejected by the very people I thought I needed to save.

When I went in and out of the house and garage and from room to room trying to catch an assailant and people looked at me strangely or asked me what was wrong, I wouldn't say. I felt helpless—it was as if the ones who tortured me moved so fast and had such control that they could do just about anything and there was nothing I could do about it.

This hallucination happened countless times and each time was as disturbing, or more so, than the last. I couldn't battle them properly, so I sank further into madness and delusion because of these hallucinations. I thank God that, at the time of this writing, I have been blessed to think differently and learned coping skills that keep me from experiencing this type of hallucination.

Writings everywhere

I could see words scribbled on the walls, on pieces of junk metal, car doors and hoods. Almost any surface. There would be random words and names. The most predominant word was 'murder'. I saw the word 'murder' scribbled everywhere.

I used to stare at objects and watch the words scramble and change. I watched and tried to figure out what the message was, but it was never clear to me. I hated the writings on the wall. They made me skeptical of the people closest to me. Often I would be with someone and think the message was about them.

This hallucination was another that had me stare into 'space' seemingly. I was looking at something very real to me. I don't remember telling very many people about this hallucination. Most people I did attempt to tell about any of my delusions treated me like I was crazy. I guess I was.

These types of delusions make you crazy. I could get lost on any surface between the writings and visions. The writings were never anything positive. Derogatory words were all I could see on these walls and objects. The mental distress from this type of thing can be life-altering. Today, I don't focus so intensely on surfaces when I see things like the disrespectful writings.

Transforming of objects

Multiple times *The Voice* warned me of my enemies. *It* would tell me where they were coming from, when they were approaching. I saw knives and guns change into paper or other objects in front of my eyes without a blink on several occasions that I recall. I always believed that the person was coming to do me harm exactly as *It* said. This was another way *It* protected me and confused my enemies. I saw people surprised when their weapons vanished. They didn't know what had happened. *It* would not allow anyone to pass with deadly threat, quelling attempts at my assassination with speed and accuracy. There was no shadow, just like magic, they lost their weapons and diverted their course.

I think that this hallucination was a defense mechanism. At times, it's difficult for me to believe that these occurrences were nothing more than delusion, because I remember them so well. The moments still seem real. I was at war and *It* would protect me from my enemies even when I couldn't do it on my own or fully understand what was happening.

This delusion was disorienting. Most of the would-be assassins were people I did not know. There were a few that I did know and they didn't say anything to me about it. I still believe there were people out to harm me and that *It* protected me. *The Voice* is with me and I don't know how to explain these things other than to call them delusion. At the same time, I cannot make myself believe that none of this happened.

I guess I'm as warped in some ways as I ever was in the height of delusion, even medicated and sober. I don't battle as much with realities anymore. God sent me *The Voice* and I will not deny Him of that. Although this 'hallucination' may seem farfetched, God is capable of anything and his creations are given power in their realms.

The truth of the matter is that being insane doesn't completely warp your perception 100% of the time. Things that are very real to me are the inexplicable phenomena that marked the existence of God in my life and the guardian army he sent to fight with me and for me.

My becoming a giant

There were times I grew big enough that I could look down at the world, into crowds and stadiums. I watched people and wasn't sure why I had grown so big. It was like the whole world was on the carpet. I saw a stadium and thousands of people making noise. I watched until I heard something disturbing on the radio. I remember I didn't want to stand up and crush anyone. So, I stayed still until the hallucination changed.

It was a strange and bewildering thought that if I moved I could crush thousands of people. I didn't see the game or event in the stadium. I could only see crowds of people waving their arms and yelling and screaming. I thought I could see the streets around the stadium and cars rushing every which way. The voices told me that if I moved I would crush them.

I remember having an overwhelming urge to pace the floor, but I didn't want to harm all the people. The radio started talking about a giant during one of these hallucinations and the voices told me they were talking about me. During these types of hallucinations, I might spend long hours staring at the floor, or try to make the hallucination stop by staring at the wall. There was always a sick movie for me on the wall and I felt trapped with nowhere to go without causing damage to innocent people. The giant delusion could be taxing.

Snakes everywhere

The snake hallucination was one of the worst and the most difficult to hide from family and friends. It started early in my sickness and never has stopped. Even medicated and sober for years I still see snakes more than anything. I would believe there were live snakes in my pillows, biting me. I had thought they were sewn into my covers. I wouldn't want to lay in the bed during these hallucinations. I could see them, transparent on the floor, or think they were in my pockets.

I tried showing my wife what I thought were snake bites from the bed. I thought people were throwing them on me. I thought they were in the attic. I thought they were in the floor boards of cars I would be riding in. I thought they were in my pockets. I even tried to get a friend to reach into my pocket and get one out once.

This is and was one of my worst delusions. I see them sometimes, today. I always wonder if I will mistake a real one for a hallucination. I saw a transparent one turn into a real one once. It became solid at the head first and formed all the way to the tip of the tail. It belonged to someone in the house I was in. The incident furthered my suspicion that they were all real. My counterpart, *It*, never said I was hallucinating the snakes. The silence would make me a believer.

This hallucination has stopped me from walking down dark roads. The snakes have appeared everywhere. Hospitals, prisons and anywhere else you can think of, I've seen them everywhere. When this first started, it was debilitating. I had a difficult time not reacting to the see-through reptiles.

Snakes are some of the longest running delusions I've had. It happened so often and in so many places I wondered if everyone was in on it. I couldn't figure out how they made them invisible or why they were taunting me with them. I often left homes and places that I visited because of the snakes.

A delusion like this makes you unsure of everything and everyone. When something like this is happening and you can't pinpoint the source or reason, everyone becomes suspect. It served to make me untrusting of some of the people that I may have been able to trust, furthering my alienation. When you believe, people are throwing snakes on you, naturally you feel unwanted.

I haven't hallucinated anyone throwing snakes on me for some time at the writing of this book, but I do see them sometimes. Fortunately, with the coping methods I've acquired, I find it easier to discard the hallucinations of reptiles. Still, it's a burden to experience these types of hallucinations.

There were other animals also. Dogs and large cats. I'm not going to go into great detail about them, because they are on the same premise that the reptiles are. The reptiles were the most predominant and that is why I made this entry about them. The hallucinations of deadly animals can make you have all types of extreme reactions. Most of the time I tried to remain calm through them, but I can't deny in the least that these visions helped to cripple and warp my mentality.

Power over others

In my sickness, there were times when I believed that I had the ability to control the minds of others. I believed that I could make people do anything. I could basically *will* them to do whatever I wanted, and they would do it. These were also very real hallucinations. I could see people doing the things I willed them to do. They would do these things in a sort of spirit realm I guess. They never seemed to remember. This was perversion. I don't want to talk about the things I made them do much. Most of it was violent.

Keep in mind these are people whom *It* told me were my enemies, or people who were trying to hurt my family, my friends or me, in my mind. Nonetheless, it's disturbing and just the memory of these delusions unsettles me. I was in some of my sickest stages when I had these hallucinations.

Imagine being so mentally sick that all you think about is war and death, then somehow you are given the ability to make your enemies do anything you could think of. Would you manifest a running chainsaw and have an enemy swallow it? Make them pull out their own eye balls? During the sickest of moments, you never know what atrocities your inner, warped mind can conjure. I don't like thinking of these things much, but for the sake of better understanding, I relay these things to you now.

My nuclear capabilities

My army was in possession of nuclear devices. If I was killed, the nukes would be set off in certain areas. *The Voice* told me that if I were to die, there would be heavy repercussions for the world. I walked through multiple areas and my army took over any place I inhabited. They would come in to occupy my current position, then to move the army and/or dominate other areas, I would walk. Wherever I went, nuclear capabilities went also.

Believing that the repercussions of my death were too massive for the enemy strongholds to afford helped me make my journeys into different sections of the city with little rest. *The Voice* guided me the whole way. The many voices of legions attempted to discourage me from my path, but I did not fail, in my mind.

Dismembered and reassembled

I would sit still and feel myself being cut to pieces. I felt my limbs being pulled apart and I felt them putting me back together. There were times when I was walking and thought my stomach had been cut open and I was dragging my intestines. There were other times when I thought the back of my head was missing or that I was disfigured.

These delusions were always when *It* would tell me my enemies had me. *It* would tell me to stay calm. *It* said my soldiers were coming. I could hear the battle. Eventually they would put me back together. This was also some sort of defense mechanism. I try not to let my mind wander to these times. I don't like to think about the things my enemies did to me. I know that it was delusion, on the level I'm on now, but at the time it was as real as anything else in my life.

Missing limbs and digits

I would see peoples' fingers or legs disappear and reappear. It happened random, but often. A girl would be on the phone in front of me and her finger would disappear. I would be walking up the street and see a man in the distance with missing legs. When I would get close, the missing body parts would reappear. This hallucination made me weary of people with missing limbs.

The sound of the saws

I COULD HEAR RUNNING SAWS. I could hear the loud and aggressive roar. My enemies were being cut to pieces. I could hear their screams and the visions would show me what was happening. It became especially disturbing when this hallucination poured over to more than my enemies. That's what the hallucination had me believe.

The saws came from all my work in my father's wood shop, I think. I used the saws all day sometimes and the voices plagued me. When I was in the height of delusion, the saws became a reoccurring and perplexing form of torture. I don't hear the saws at the time of this writing and for that I'm grateful.

Rolling blackouts

I thought the lights were going out because of me. Once I was walking and every street light I walked underneath seemed to shut off. When I got to my destination, there was no power. I thought it was because of the war, a tactic of my enemies or of my own army.

The blackouts were a strange delusion that would come and go. The way it affected me was that when I thought it was happening, I wouldn't want to go many places. I'd usually find an abandoned house and hoped that the people I knew still had power. I wasn't sure which way to turn until this delusion would subside.

When you think that your presence is a cause for discomfort with your family and friends, the last thing you want is to be the reason they have no power, amongst other things. *The Voice* would get angry with me and tell me to keep moving. The hordes of other voices would laugh at me and mock me for not wanting to move.

Eventually, I would make my way from whatever location and the blackouts didn't last long. Most of the time it was a short-lived delusion. Other times, I lived in actual residences for weeks with no power, no water and no food.

Afterword on hallucinations

The preceding are merely some of the delusions I've experienced. There are intricate details to each that I could not take time to expound on, for there are things I'd still rather not talk about. I'm not 'all the way there' yet. I do think it's important to catalogue and examine some of the more dominant hallucinations, and that's what I've done here in summary form. These delusions were complex and still threaten to haunt me to this day.

6 MENTAL POLLUTION AND BODY ART

I have so many disturbing thoughts daily. I used to argue with the voices and curse at my thoughts. I was a 'basket case' until I found some coping methods that have been working for me. Before I acquired the habit of writing and other mental defenses and releases, I habitually paced for hours, consumed in negativity. I still pace around, but focus on positive thoughts these days.

The voices try to make me believe that people are against me. They try to say derogatory things about people to me while I'm holding conversations, and I try to ignore them so I can communicate properly. They tell me stories that I turn into books now. I no longer let them run amok. I put them to work. When they say something, I don't say 'fuck you' anymore to the voices. Instead, I say 'throw that overboard' to myself and I visualize myself taking negative thoughts and ideas and throwing them from the side of a ship into the sea. This method works for me. It's an exercise I pulled from *The Power of Positive Thinking*, by Norman Vincent Peale.

The voices convinced me that people were trying to impersonate me and I began getting more and more tattoos that were clearly visible and made it harder for anyone to pretend to be me. I started with my neck. I put my nickname, then I put my daughter's name on the other side. Then the tear drops for the fallen. My arms are covered with art that has meaning to me, but the real purpose of those tattoos is to function like a license plate. There are spider webs above and below the left eye on my face that I tattooed in the mirror in a state of delusion and paranoia. They mean 'keep one eye open'. Paranoia has always been my ugliest friend.

My legs are tattooed to symbolize a walk through Hell. My arms are tattooed to represent my fight with evil. My hands are gloved for danger. There are over thirty words on my body. All the tattoos have meaning. My chest is a depiction of the battle field. The meanings associated with my tattoos are not obvious. You wouldn't know these things by casual observation. And there's more to it: I just like ink. I would like to be covered from head to toe. Recently, I've decided to be more conservative for the sake of business.

I go through so many thoughts and mental scenarios in a day that I could write hundreds of books and, eventually, I most likely will. The difficult thing is distinguishing delusion from reality. Some of the things that I imagine and see are so real to me that they become hard to debunk in my mind.

There's something inside me, such an imbalance,

that *It* never lets me be. I must take medication to think straight. I must use coping mechanisms and tell myself that certain things are not real or I *will* wander off into delusion again. The plight of someone with schizoaffective disorder is very real. You may be tempted to dismiss my problems as only *thoughts*, and you may control your own so well that it seems trivial, but the disease is not trivial. At times, it is debilitating. If it were not for others like my family, friends, doctors, social worker, probation officer, counselors and psychiatrist, I would probably still be roaming the streets lost to the world or dead.

When deranged thoughts become more predominant than reality, it's difficult to come back. The hallucinations I covered in the last chapter are by no means an exhaustive catalog of what I experience during the heights of sickness. I'll do my best to explain as much as I'm willing to. It's difficult to catalogue everything. Some things are so complex that they almost can't be explained. I am trying to share my world with whomever will listen or read in hopes that it may help someone—or else aid those who are interested in understanding this disease.

People didn't know what to think of me

When people don't know what to think of you or what might be going through your head, they can't make an accurate decision about the things that ail you. Most people simply aren't qualified or capable of dealing with a person who is consumed by schizoaffective disorder. A person with this disease can seem normal one day, week, or month, then be completely out of sorts in just moments. With stress, the symptoms worsen and without medication there is no balance. Someone who seemed normal one day suddenly becomes distant and volatile, or unresponsive.

Communication, bodily and verbal, becomes stilted during the deterioration of the mental faculties. As I've said, the use of illicit narcotics serves to further increase deterioration of mental and motor skills. So, when someone is in a situation such that they are offered illegal drugs more often than food and are homeless or living in high risk environments, it's almost like there are no breaks. Mentally ill people are more susceptible to using illicit narcotics. We try to escape our delusional world, only to slip further into insanity.

The thought that a prescribed pill coupled with sobriety could enable you to function properly is hard to believe for someone in the throes of insanity. Hallucinations are difficult to escape when you're schizoaffective, especially when using illicit substances that are known to induce symptoms of schizophrenia in a 'normal' subject. If a person is schizoaffective with bi-polar and advanced psychosis, they might be more susceptible to believing what the voices are telling them, and less likely to listen to the explanation of a doctor or the people and world around them.

A difficult aspect of the disease is that to have any chance at a 'regular' life, you must be willing to accept help and do what it takes to make changes. It's more than taking a prescribed pill, it's the willingness to be open with family, friends and doctors. It's all about caring, choosing to associate with caring people, if possible. It's the mindset the patient adopts that determines the quality of life.

Without a willingness to change one's mindset and association, you lose. The inability to recognize the depths of your sickness or to understand how your lifestyle can be improved leaves you chasing self-prescribed cures in the belief that there is no hope. Refusing to talk about the issues we face—these are the things that will impede recovery and relief.

The people in the lives of the schizoaffective drug addict will assume that the problem is simply drugs. Before diagnosis, the ill person will also use drugs as an excuse and escape. It's comforting to have a scapegoat for the afflicted and the relations of the afflicted. It's almost more acceptable for someone to be a drug addict and experience the types of hallucinations and delusions I catalogued, than it is for it to be an integral—life long—part of the person.

Things would be much simpler for me if I could give up bad habits and be perfectly fine. It isn't that simple. If a person is not diagnosed, the cycle will continue. Drug abuse, delirium and alienation.

Granted, a patient is much better off without the use of illegal narcotics, but not healed. The brain does not stop working in overdrive when the illness is peaking and although at times symptoms may seem to lie dormant to the observing individual, what's happening in the mind is critical in nature. Without medication, counseling and some kind of support system, the afflicted one almost always follows some sort of destructive path.

It's not just drugs. There were times I thought I could escape the voices by changing locations. I've gone as far as stealing cars to get away from an area, thinking that the voices wouldn't follow. I was wrong. I was always wrong. The voices may seem to change, but they always follow and become just as bad, or may even increase at the new location. Understand, it's difficult to believe that all the hallucinations, auditory and visual, aren't coming from somewhere or something external.

Believing that the things I experienced were somehow external, I attempted to escape the chaos frequently, trying different methods. Driving, walking, waiting until no one was physically around and not letting anyone know where I was going. The delusions followed and the voices and visions persisted. These things are unexplainable and I didn't want to explain it to anyone, because I didn't know who was in on it.

That kind of thinking further alienated me from everyone and kept me from getting the help I needed. I thought about telling the different people who came into my life and tried to help me. I couldn't. I didn't want to put them in danger. The voices told me of the terrible things they would do if I spoke up. Visions polluted my mind with things that I did not want to believe. I would go to people's homes that I had the visions of. I wanted to ask them if something was happening to them. Sometimes I did. The people I did ask or try to protect in my own weird way always made me feel insane.

I suppose I was extremely insane. Today it's not hard to understand why others treated me the way that they did. When it was happening, I couldn't understand. My grasp on reality was so loose that I could have been anywhere, in any situation, and I would have gone through these types of oddities. Whether good or bad, sober or under the influence, I did not relate, because something was happening with me that was yet undiscovered.

When average people confront this disease in you, they probably think you are going to be lost to the world for the rest of your life. Some give up on you completely and others only help because they feel it's their duty. Since I've gained what I can of my sanity back, I've been told by numerous people that they believed I would be messed up for life. I've even been told by one, and assume it is the same for a few, that they thought they were above me intellectually. They considered me to be retarded mentally, I guess. Someone to be pitied.

Inside my head, I was never mentally retarded. My brain worked quickly and with complexity. What gave the impression that I was slow were my poor verbal, social and motor skills. I know how easy it would be for someone to think that a person who is in the height of schizoaffective disorder must be shy on intellect. I had trouble keeping up with things, and lost pretty much everything I'd collected over the years. We tend to make poor decisions or simply leave things and people behind when we're mentally deranged.

I can only speak of my experience directly, and I hope that it will touch someone who needs to hear that they are not alone, or to open the eyes of those who are ignorant of this affliction and to possibly help some who actively seek knowledge on these subjects. All that is in this book are my experiences. Not everyone will have the same walk. Everyone won't have the same catalysts, hallucinations or delusions. To some extent, the condition has one thing in common for everyone. The disease makes it extremely difficult to live and prosper without help.

The help I received may not have seemed adequate to me when I was receiving it, but there was help. I wasn't being receptive. My family and the hospitals did not give up on me. When I began to seek help, it was there. Once again, if the patient isn't willing and receptive to the help offered, it is unlikely that much can be done.

When I was admitted to the hospital, over and over, I would not talk to them. I ate the food and was eventually set free without the care I needed, because I would not open up to the people who asked me, "What's wrong? What's happening with you?"

There's crowding in the mental wards. Either you get diagnosed, committed, or set free. I'm not sure why I was set free so many times without diagnosis. It doesn't matter to me today. I think I had to go through what I was going through to become the person that I am today. I like the person I am today.

Although I hear the voices and see things occasionally, I think my life is better than it has been in a long time. I owe it to family, friends and institutions. I know, most people hate the institutions. They only see the negative side. For me they were rehabilitation havens, at times. They took me away from drugs and the kind of chaos that came with living from place to place. An organized, clean and calculated life.

I wouldn't put myself there today. I love my freedom. The various times I found myself institutionalized were usually at just the right moments in my life. I was running myself into an early grave. Insanity ate away at the core of my being. I needed the change. I needed the staff in program units and other inmates/patients. Interaction and mindset change are the keys to my successes today. If I were bitter, or chose to ignore this truth, I'd lose what makes my life so great now.

I didn't like the institutions much while I was there. I just can't deny that they made a positive impact on my life. It wasn't just sitting around in a hospital room or prison cell. I'm talking about groups and activities, programs. Those things helped me become the person I am. They bettered me at the core—where I was rotting.

It was a combination of the people in my life and the places I've been that have made me the person I am today. I am forever thankful. It doesn't matter as much anymore that there were points in my life that seemed hopeless; I don't dwell on those periods. It doesn't matter that no one could know the exact horrors I experienced, mentally. I don't want them to know completely. What I want is to live a life of purpose. I want to be healthy, mentally and physically. The people in my life and the places I've been, people I've left behind—have all contributed to who I am. I find my freedom in writing these days. My life is a good one now. I was on my own path and, even with help, ultimately, we all must save ourselves by wanting to be saved. Otherwise, we will always be in the dark, wallowing in sickness.

There were many times I wanted to be helped, but suffered my disease in silence. The hard part is breaking the hold of the delusions that have you thinking there's no hope. Fight the delusion that makes you believe you can't get better or ask for help. I don't care who you are. If you're living life with schizophrenia/schizoaffective disorder, seek knowledge about your disease, and seek counsel. Start by talking to those closest to you. The hardest part is change. If it seems like no one knows what to do with you, they probably don't. You must let them know.

The day I began opening up was the day the doctor said, "We can help you now." Some of the most important words in my lifetime.

Life with minimal interaction

Being socially withdrawn and sick was like living in exile. Few people try to spend time with someone who doesn't communicate well and behaves strangely. I would find myself staying with friends or family and would often hope in vain that someone would invite me to ride with them or do something together. It happened on occasion, but most of the time, I sat alone with my thoughts and voices until *It* directed me to walk away.

I wonder now whether many people missed me when I was gone. I wonder if they were relieved when I left. I'm sure they were relieved some of the time. I was consumed with delusion, so I can imagine that when I was gone it was less awkward. Being socially awkward isn't something I have gotten completely over. Prison helped me with my communication skills some. I participated daily in the last program I was in.

We could stand up to share struggles in the morning meeting in the Residential Drug Abuse Program (RDAP) prison unit. When I had a struggle, I would stand up in front of about a hundred inmates and talk about whatever I was going through. The inmates could give me feedback and I found it therapeutic, plus it built bonds. Sometimes after I had shared a struggle, inmates would come to me and talk after the meeting was over.

I felt that the way my peers approached me was helpful, so whenever I had occasion to offer feedback to an inmate during a group session, after the group session was over I would aim to have a real one-on-

one conversation with whomever it was. Doing this helped me become a better communicator and get to know some of the inmates well. Before long, I had plenty of people to talk to in the unit.

I think being accepted socially is a difficult milestone for the mentally ill. When your mind is polluted with voices and you suffer delusions, it's hard to move past that. I'm not sure I'll ever be totally free of my awkwardness, but I make a stronger effort today than I have in the past decade before the RDAP unit. I think if there were more programs in the various institutions that promoted community involvement, the benefits for the mentally ill and the antisocial in general would be great.

7 MY TIME IN INSTITUTIONS

John Peter Smith, Fort Worth, Texas

The tenth-floor psychiatric ward of John Peter Smith Hospital (JPS) housed me more times than I can remember. I finally opened up to a doctor there, after multiple fruitless visits of silence. I was always in such a mental state when visiting there that I do not remember any of the nurses' and doctor's names. There were so many. After observation and being moved into housing, they would interact with me more. The nurses and psychiatrists were all caring; they nurtured my spirit and health. There were groups to attend and opportunities to interact. This is where I was finally diagnosed.

Trinity Springs Pavilion

After I was diagnosed, I was admitted to the Trinity Springs Pavilion on JPS grounds. The programs there were all helpful. I liked being there more than anywhere else because the patients were easier to interact with. I enjoyed listening and joining in activities at this location. The staff there are all caring and I know they wanted to help.

Places like these were lifesavers. Being in the hospital could be a negative or positive experience depending on your mindset while you're there. If you are consumed with hallucinations and delusion, there isn't much that anyone can do until you begin to become open about the things that ail you. Contrary to what the hallucinations may have you believe, like mine did, that everyone can hear your thoughts and are aware of what's happening with you—it's just not true.

To benefit from the services of a mental hospital, you must come out of your own mind and express yourself. It wasn't until I let the doctor know that I was hearing voices and seeing things that I could receive help. The longer you wait and believe what the negative voices tell you, the worse you will become. Eventually, you could even be committed without diagnosis if you are perceived as a threat to others or yourself.

Parkland hospital, Dallas, Texas

I was admitted to Parkland several times. I went to their psychiatric facility and while there, they noticed I was malnourished, as usual after an episode. They gave me double portions of food and helped me stabilize on my medications. The doctors and nurses at this facility were also very helpful.

The times I was admitted to Parkland and would not speak were unproductive. I would be released back into the streets upon leaving the observation room. I remember the kind of hell that I experienced on several of my visits—I wanted to talk about it, but the voices, visions and delusions kept me silent.

Had I spoken to the doctors at Parkland in the

beginning of my hospitalizations into the mental ward, I wonder how much sooner I could have become healthy. After my diagnosis at JPS, when I moved back to Dallas, I was admitted into Parkland hospital again. The experience was intense because of my ailments, but the staff and doctors seemed to know me and how to deal with me better.

I was put in the Greenbay Ward and everyone treated me very well. When I was released a couple of weeks later, I was once again 'stable'. The difference an accurate diagnosis makes is astounding. Due to the hospitals and doctors in my life since my diagnosis, my life has enjoyed a considerable increase in comfort and quality.

Hutchins State Jail, Dallas, Texas

Although prison isn't the ideal environment, there were some positive things about the jails and prisons I've been incarcerated in. Interacting with other inmates and taking a drug program at Hutchins was good. There are a lot of things about the state prison system that I do not like. They don't have an abundance of activities and the living conditions could be better. The buildings are like warehouses for humans. I believe that Texas state penitentiaries should be improved; in particular, they should be geared more towards rehabilitation and re-entry to society.

On the better side of the state discussion: Being incarcerated there opened my eyes to what I didn't want my life to be like. Spending time in this place helped me gain focus and get healthy. There's time to exercise and there used to be three meals a day, every day. I returned to Hutchins after my first stay. Not because I liked the food or company, although the company wasn't always bad.

I haven't been able to hold a job throughout my life for more than a couple of weeks or months. When I was undiagnosed and un-medicated, I had issues dealing with people daily. My sleeping patterns were erratic and I often hallucinated and was plagued with unhealthy thoughts. All these things combined made it difficult to commit my services.

I turned to crime, mostly because it was always there, no matter what state of mind I was in. It came easily and naturally to me for many years and I didn't feel like I had to answer to anyone or be anywhere that I didn't want to. I'm not an active criminal today. My life has completely changed.

Although I still have a difficult time, I run my own company and my successes and failures sit squarely on my own shoulders. I do work with people and I enjoy work and good company. The criminal lifestyle is an unhealthy one. I see it as a hindrance and as irresponsible, unethical behavior to do anything illegal. I don't even like speeding.

Middleton Unit, Abilene, Texas

Middleton—a state prison—was a sweaty and altogether different experience for me. I had issues with a guard during intake. He was rude, aggressive and disrespectful. I kept my cool, and all my movements and words were calculated and deliberate so that the situation wouldn't escalate. I had decided to write books previously while in county jail, so I was happy to be somewhere I could start my first novel. After the initial problem with the guard, I didn't have many more problems. They made me a dorm janitor at night, so I could stay up and write in the middle of the night when everyone slept and the dorm was quiet.

I was transferred from Middleton into federal custody after about six months in the dorm. All my writing for that period was put into my property. I never could get my property sent to anyone. I sent numerous letters to the prison about my property, but received no reply—ultimately, my property from this period was lost. Middleton is my story of perseverance with writing. I didn't quit because I lost my first novel. I have written multiple books, short stories and poems since leaving that unit. Never give up.

Don't Quit

When things go wrong, as they sometimes will,

When the road you're trudging seems all uphill,

When the funds are low and the debt is high,

And you want to smile, but you have to sigh,

When care is pressing you down a bit,

Rest if you must—but don't you quit.

~ Clinton Howell

F.C.I. Jail Unit, Fort Worth, Texas

At the federal holdover, I was surprised how much better the federal system was than state. They had computers to use for email, managing visitation lists, adding phone time, checking for money on your books, and a label machine for letters. You could add any number to your phone list in minutes. I didn't have many people to call, but it made things less complicated for those times when I did, as opposed to the state system in which the inmate is totally dependent on paperwork and the actions (or inaction) of corrections officers for accomplishing all mundane tasks.

The federal lockup had a library full of books that anyone could get, read and return. We had radios and microwave ovens. The food was better and the guards treated you more humanely, with respect—that was my experience. There're always a few bad ones in the bunch. That's with any group of people, in my opinion.

There were also multiple televisions. I didn't watch much TV, but it was nice that there weren't many fights about which channels to watch. I had a friend there from the free world. It was good to see him every day, and we were even cell mates for a while. The caliber of inmates seemed better, also. Maybe because there wasn't such a gladiator vibe. Everyone was waiting to go to court.

I did get into a fight, but I believe it was unavoidable. The guy couldn't control his mouth with me and thought I was a pushover. It ended up bloody, but if I had it my way, I'd never have to fight. That's why when I raise my arms, the tattoos read 'Hard Life'. I usually only fight out of necessity. I've never been one to just push people around or put my hands on them for no reason.

Out of the hundred or so inmates in this holdover, he was the only one I had a problem with. The rest of the guys were always helpful when I needed it and we pretty much got along like family. I paced the top tier a lot. There were a few who liked to walk and talk with me. Some of them wanted to write books also. We'd talk about life and books, things we wanted to do when we went home, or our families.

United States Prison High Security, Beaumont, Texas

Because of my long record, I was sent to a high security prison. They had nicknamed the place Bloody Beaumont at one time. From what I'm told, it was the most violent federal prison in the country for some years. While I was there, stabbings and fights occurred regularly. More than I cared for. Being there sucked in a lot of ways. Some ways, it was good.

They had three recreational yards. No. 1 yard was the best. It had hobby classes and work out equipment, handball courts, basketball courts, Bochy ball, pool tables, ping pong tables, shuffleboard tables—and you could have your picture taken there for family, friends, or pen pals, if you had a ticket that could be purchased at commissary.

The chow hall was big, containing multiple tables for groups to sit and eat. The food was good compared to TDCJ[2].

There were job opportunities for inmates and the institution paid you to work. It helps a lot to get paid a few bucks a month when you have little else coming in. So even in a violent federal penitentiary, it was better than any TDCJ facility. Most of the time, the violence didn't bother me too much. I had been exposed to and hallucinated such extreme violence throughout my life that I'm not very sensitive to it. That doesn't mean I like it. It just doesn't rattle my

---

[2] Texas Department of Criminal Justice, *i.e.*, State Prisons.

cage very hard. I've been desensitized to a degree.

I don't advocate prison, its environments or the way we are treated in most facilities. Overall the experience of being held against your will is usually a pretty bad one. There is an endless list of things that could be more productive than time in prison. The federal system is a step up, but I still believe it's flawed and there are a lot of people who are serving unjust sentences. Non-violent crimes such as drug convictions shouldn't be as heavy on time. I saw a lot of non-violent offenders who had spent decades— even some who were serving life sentences—in a place where they would see very little progress.

I know that I did the best I could to utilize the time I had there. I spent hours each day writing and studying. I was received into a program unit that allowed me to work on my behavior and mentality toward others. The RDAP (Residential Drug Abuse Program) made a huge difference in the time I spent in prison and in my life. Dr. M. M. LeFever and the Drug Treatment Specialists (DTS) worked with me and numerous inmates to improve our cognitive thinking and intelligence. I feel blessed to have attended and completed the program.

I don't think I would be having the kind of successes I'm having today if it weren't for RDAP. I know some of the guys didn't take it as seriously as I did, and that's their prerogative. For me it was a chance to learn some things that could help me be better in society, for my family, friends and people who invested so much time trying to pull me from the depths of Hell.

Making an effort and taking the program seriously was the least I could do for my loved ones. I learned to hold myself to a higher standard. I gained resolve to eliminate unhealthy relationships. I developed coping skills, social skills and so much more. Although Dr. Lefever was steadfast in the success of the program and at times difficult to deal with, she is one of the greatest women I have ever known. Watching her and the way she operated, gave me great insight into the world of integrity and strategic control.

Following is the text of a speech I wrote as my class representative upon our graduation from the RDAP:

In the beginning:

I was nervous about getting accepted into the program, and even worried whether I was going to be able to complete it. I felt that my interview went horribly, and that this might not be the place for me. They moved me into the unit and it was like another world compared to the unit I was living in before. What immediately stood out were the paintings. I like art, and it gave me a good vibe. After interacting with some of the guys, and observing how things were done, my anxiety began to dissipate.

Rules:

The rules here are strict compared to anywhere else I've been. At first, this bothered me, and maybe it bothered a large majority of the group here, given most of us haven't spent our time paying close attention to the rules. I have a better understanding now of the rules that are enforced, because I want to succeed, not only in this program, but also in life in general. I've come to the understanding that, even if I believe something is petty, there will still be consequences for breaking the rules.

Struggles:

I've had my fair share of struggles. Through my struggles inside and outside of this unit, I've had support from my peers who are too numerous to address individually at the moment. I'm sure most of my classmates feel the same. Making it through this program and life successfully is a group effort in the least. I cannot say I would be as well off mentally as I am at this moment if it were not for my peers. On behalf of myself and everyone you may have helped or will help in the future, I would like to personally say thank you to each of you, along with Dr. LeFever, DTS Sam, Frank, Germosen, and Mr. Good, for your dedication to this community.

Dedication:

My classmates and I have been dedicated to change and progress through the phases, in the face of considerable odds

> *and setbacks. Each of us has chosen a thoughtful phrase or quote with personal meaning to our recovery to share with you today.*
>
> **Quote:** *"Well done is better than well said." Benjamin Franklin*
>
> *~ June 2014 RDAP unit, Beaumont USP.*

If you gather from my speech that this unit and the people in it changed my life, you are correct. I gave this speech in front of about a hundred inmates and some prison staff at my graduation. There were great incentives to keep me going in the program, and in the end, it's the program that is the reward. We practiced caring, gratitude, honesty, open-mindedness, objectivity, humility, responsibility, and willingness. We studied *Rational Self-Analysis*. We learned more about respect and forgiveness.

This speech, along with my certificate of completion, is framed and mounted on the wall beside my desk. I will not forget how far I've come in recovery and in life, with my illness and drug addiction. Dr. LeFever assigned me exercises; for instance, writing out positive affirmations. When it was time for my mental health reviews, she would look them over and give me feedback. She gave me books on coping skills. I never went into detail about the tragedies in my life with her. If I told her I felt depressed or I was seeing things on the walls, she did her best to find active solutions.

I think all prisons in the U.S. should be run like

federal penitentiaries. I think they should all have the 'luxuries' and programs, with incentives to do well. My experience in the RDAP unit was intense. I was ecstatic to leave when my day came, but I cannot and will not deny that the RDAP unit had a lasting, positive effect on me as a person. I believe I am a better person. I know I can be a productive citizen. I owe a good part of the confidence I have today to that program and the people in it, inmates and staff alike.

I rarely missed my medication while in the unit. When I did, I would have a sleepless night and the hallucinations would start around 10 p.m. and continue until I received my dose the following afternoon and went to sleep. Most of this was due to being locked in a box, in a high stress situation. My cellmate would always encourage me to take my meds and he always knew when I didn't take them. Living in a small cell with someone, you tend to pick up on more than those who only interact with you periodically throughout the day.

I paced the cell a lot and it got me into more than a few arguments and even up-close confrontations. My last cell mate and a few before him were understanding. Although they were understanding, I know it was difficult—especially during lockdowns. I would pace the most during lockdown. When I say pace, I don't mean for a few minutes. I paced for hours. Without medication or with medication, I paced. Now imagine I missed my medication and can't sleep. I would pace at the end of the bed all night sometimes. It had to be frustrating for my cellmates.

The worse times for me in prison were the times

that my pacing caused serious problems with others. My compulsion was hard to control. I would start doing it before I realized it on occasion. I pace today, at home. Sometimes for hours. I have a space in my room big enough to make a few strides and I go back and forth while listening to music and thinking. It calms me. If it was up to me I would always have had my own, single cell, where I wouldn't bother anyone.

Out in the prison unit, I paced the top tier so much and ate so little that I dropped from 180lbs to 148lbs only months into my sentence. I used to be a picky eater. I wouldn't eat vegetables, onions, green peppers, peas and carrots. People started noticing my weight and telling me I looked sick. I didn't get much money for commissary and I knew I had to do something about my health. I was burning too many calories without enough fuel. I didn't stop pacing; instead, I started eating everything I could. I am no longer a picky eater. I'm 230lbs today and climbing. Don't worry, I frequent the gym.

I had a job in the kitchen that got me out of the unit each day, and friends on the shift with me. It was good. The hours that the kitchen was clear, I had a large area to walk. My friends liked to walk with me sometimes and talk. They'll probably never know what that meant to me. During chow, I saw almost everyone from the compound about twice a day. Sometimes I worked breakfast and lunch, and other times I worked lunch and dinner. I didn't hustle out of the kitchen, meaning that I refused to pilfer things from work. I was too focused on my program to risk any nonsense. There were a few people who couldn't understand my resolve. I never let what others may or may not have thought of me stop me from achieving my goals. Going home was always first in my thoughts and more important to me than gaining trinkets or maintaining a bad boy image.

Overall, I think most of the compound liked me. I minded my own business more than some and I tried not to get involved in political issues every time they arose. I've never been the one to follow a crowd blindly. I'd rather lead myself and fail, than to follow another and fail. I do believe the old adage that you must know how to follow in order to lead, but you need to choose whom to follow wisely. I chose my battles cautiously and went through orthodox channels for dealing with issues that required group consensus, but I am no sheep.

So, with the program, writing, exercise, work and the glue that holds it all together—medication—I've done well. It was a long and bumpy road. I went through hell, mentally and physically, to have the pleasure of writing this for you. I was lost and never gave up. I persisted and have been granted freedom. The disease no longer rules me. My change of mindset has given me the confidence to chase my dreams and fulfill my goals.

The Volunteers of America federal halfway house

When I was released from the Beaumont Federal Prison, I rode a bus to Fort Worth. I had a bed waiting in a federal halfway house where I would spend the next six months. I was nervous about making it through. I knew that I would be required to have a job. I wasn't sure I'd be able to get one.

Getting a job ended up being the least of my problems. The prison sent two types of pills in the prescription bottle for my anti-psychotic medication.

It was a Friday when they noticed that there were 30 extra pills and they didn't all look the same. They pulled my medication and I could not sleep without it or suppress my hallucinations. By the end of the weekend I was experiencing full blown psychosis.

I had to be hospitalized the next week, on Christmas day. My children had come to visit me and had to watch the ambulance take me away. I was sad inside watching their faces as paramedics wheeled me away on a gurney. It took several weeks to stabilize. Going through psychosis in the type of place I was in is bad news. People were handing me cups of coffee and giving me food. I'm convinced I was drugged. When I returned to the halfway house from the hospital, they moved me upstairs to a room near the front desk so that they could watch me more closely. They also asked the guys in my room to look out for me and make sure I took my medication and was okay.

One man in particular became a great friend. He always reminded me about things that needed doing and would talk to me every day. I will always be thankful to him for being a real friend in my time of need. Brian Parker, in my opinion, is of top caliber and I will always consider him my true friend.

I eventually found a job. Life at the halfway house wasn't what I expected, but there were some good people there. It was co-ed and the women, inmates and staff, were nice. Most of the women were beautiful physically and otherwise. I like beautiful women with great personalities because they make the days more bearable. The atmosphere and diversity were a nice change.

When the hallucinations subsided, I contacted one

of the women who wrote me while I was in prison. Before long she started visiting me. She's such a special person, and it was nice to have someone other than family who would go out of their way to visit me. I will probably always love her for her sacrifice for the rest of my life. She would fly all the way from New York to Texas to see me and just spend time with me.

My family visited often. My father and daughter, son and sister, niece and nephew. I was really beginning to feel the love and I think that has made a considerable difference in my view of life. I didn't concern myself with what I had no control over, and I enjoyed the company I kept.

I went to aftercare meetings at a place called Phoenix; they were great. The counselors listened and gave feedback. They were a good support system and the other participants were great, also. I liked talking with all of them. If I lived closer I would visit them again, and someday I probably will visit. All these people that have made an effort in my life in the last five years make me want to make a difference for others. Perhaps some people, when finding themselves in a situation such as a halfway house, would look at these social groups as a sort of punishment. For me they were just what they were designed to be, therapy—although I admit, I was very happy to be done with them when time came to be released.

8 MY PAROLE

My father had a place for me to go when I left the halfway house. If it weren't for him I would have been homeless. I would probably be on social security, because it's difficult for me to hold a regular job with my condition. He helped me start a business and I can work at my own pace. My father is my savior. I was nervous about coming home. Maybe even more nervous than going to prison, at first, but I was also excited.

My focus is success. I worried about what kind of probation/parole officer I would get. I knew that I was willing to live clean and healthy, so that wasn't much of a concern. My concern was whether the people who were going to be monitoring me would be nice and helpful people. I didn't want to have to be paired with abrasive people because with my disease conflict is always magnified.

The probation officer whom I am fortunate to have in my life at the time of this writing is perceptive about things that could cause me to be derailed. I look forward to our visits, because I believe that she is there to help. It's not what most prisoners think. When you're trying to do the right thing, and living life the best you can, I think the officers see that. I also think that they can see when you're trying to get over, or going down the wrong path. That's when there's problems.

What we don't realize when we're doing the wrong thing is how much damage we do to our relationships, whether it be work, family, community or someone put in place to make sure our re-entry is going smoothly. I try to welcome the hurdles and do what I can to get off papers as soon as possible, with as minimal complication as possible. My goal is success, in all areas of my life.

I was assigned a counselor soon after my release. I enjoyed my visits with him. It was therapeutic. I like to think of him as a friend, because he was always willing to listen to my concerns and made sure my mind was where it needed to be. To me, he is my friend. It's surprising how many great people there are who are willing to make an effort to see that I'm thinking straight and staying on track.

About probation, I guess you could look at it one of two ways: You can think of it as a burden, and say, "I can't stand this. I want to do my own thing. I don't need this crap." Or you could say, "I screwed up and now I have to do this to make it to the next level of freedom. I'm going to make the best of this. I want to be successful. I want a good life. If being looked after for a while is what it takes, I'm going to make the best of it."

I don't endorse prison. I don't think the system is perfect. I will be glad to be 'off the leash'. One thing

I know for sure—when you live wrong, you're bound to face consequences. But one of the things I'm looking forward to is to be finally off paper, out of the probation system and truly free. I want to have the ability to travel freely. I'd like to go to New York and California, without worries. Travel to different countries. Not worry about getting violations and being sent back to prison for doing any of the little things that others don't have the threat of years subtracted from their free lives for. Not that I'm going to do anything much different than I do now besides travel and stay out of trouble the best I can.

Being mentally ill, I am happy that there are people who're concerned with my health. For a long time, I didn't have many people who cared if I was wandering the streets. People outside of my immediate family being genuinely concerned that I'm on my meds and progressing, that's a good thing, no matter who they are.

You don't have to be mentally ill to benefit from social services. If you are, these people could be life savers. Overall, the system hasn't been cruel to me. Sometimes I felt like a caged animal inside a cell, but my experiences with the people outside of prison have been uplifting at the time of this writing. My experiences are derived from willingness to stay medicated, being sober and focusing on my responsibilities.

It could be easy to get off track. Without much effort, I could screw up. I like making the effort it takes to live right. The more I do the right thing, the easier it is to do, just like doing the wrong thing. When you're schizoaffective, doing the wrong thing puts you in a place in your mind you don't want to be.

I'm compulsive about walking a straight line today.

If I were to get off my medication, there would be no way I could function and keep up with everything. My probation officer knows it and she's always inquiring about my mentality and medications. I'm sure if I hadn't been through all that I've been through, the extra attention could be unsettling. After everything I've experienced, I welcome the attention.

A genuine desire to have better for myself and succeed makes me understand with a greater clarity and open mind that my success and quality of life has a lot to do with my willingness to accept that I need to watch my mentality and associations closely. I've achieved a lot and there's so much more I want to do. I can't ignore my responsibilities and expect to achieve everything that I want. Being on paper will pass like everything else, but to truly succeed, I will never be able to neglect my mental health again.

I believe the key is how you perceive the situation you're in. If you think negative things, you will manifest negativity. If you perceive things to be a major hindrance, they will become one. Being schizoaffective amplifies positive and negative moods. It's what you focus on during the ups and downs that will determine the quality of your life. That's how it is for me.

As is our confidence, so is our capacity. ~ William Hazlitt

Support system

A support system is important for someone who is mentally ill. I keep returning to this theme because it's such an integral part of recovery and success for someone with schizophrenia/schizoaffective disorder.

I just wrote about my probation officer and counselors in the previous section and I mentioned some of my cellmates and friends. I'd like to go into further detail about my family and friends. I'd like to express the quality of life I have today, as compared to when I didn't know how to communicate and no one knew I had a serious mental condition.

When no one knew I had a detrimental illness, they pretty much shunned me. Sometimes they would leave me sitting in the corner staring at walls, or maybe they would attempt to drop me off away from them, when I had nowhere to go. Numerous times this was the situation.

I would show up somewhere they hadn't seen me in weeks or months. If they let me in, I didn't communicate. Maybe if I did communicate, I would say something disturbing. Usually they would find ways to get rid of me. Sometimes I even acted like I had somewhere to go because I knew they wanted to get rid of me. I walked for days and rarely changed clothes or showered. The voices and visions were my only companions most days and nights, even when I was in a group of people.

Various people would take me in and a lot of times offer me nothing but a place to sit. In some of these places I didn't want to sleep even if I could. Other places, when I did get to sleep, I woke in as bad a condition as before I'd slept. They might drop me off at a hospital, but I would be released in days and had nowhere to go, no one to call and no one who would take me in.

I was on my own and too sick to do anything about my situation. I feel for the people I see wandering the streets today. I know some of them are severely ill and have no one to help them in the ways they need help. I know. The ones who are mentally ill can't find a way to a better place. If they're anything like me, they feel cursed.

I remember my body feeling as though it were eating itself from hunger. I often wished I could find food somewhere, anywhere. I couldn't bring myself to eat out of the dumpster, but it was a reoccurring thought. I did whatever I could to get food, even if it meant stealing. I didn't steal from family or friends. The voices ate away at me along with my hunger. The visions tormented me to the point that I couldn't rest, wherever I was. When I was in someone's home I rarely walked into the kitchen and ate on my own or expressed my hunger. Sometimes people were perceptive and other times I walked away in the same condition I arrived.

There were times I'd make it to a family member's home and they would want to get rid of me almost immediately. If a family member or friend took me in for the night, most of them wanted me gone by the next day. I hallucinated Hell, but being alienated from everyone you know is hell for real. I wished all the madness inside me would end. I wished I could be like other people. I didn't feel human.

I would think about suicide a lot. I wondered if people would be alright with that, if they would miss me. I could envision myself jumping off bridges into traffic, or cutting myself open. I walked from Dallas to Grand Prairie down the highway and thought about jumping in front of cars.

Being mentally ill without diagnosis or support is living on the edge of death. It is a walk through Hell.

Today is different. My father is a big part of why

it's so different. He visited me at the halfway house along with my sister, son, daughter, niece, nephew and girlfriend at the time. They are the people who mean the most in my life, because they showed me they cared and they support me. If it wasn't for my father, I don't know where I'd be.

My children call me and visit with me often. There is no greater joy for me than to be in the presence of my children. My nephew likes to spend time with me. We hang out and do things together a lot. My niece always runs up to hug me when she sees me. My sister, her husband and my mother are three of the people who have showed me support before and after my diagnosis, more so after. They are still supportive at the time of this writing and I'm fortunate to have them.

The difference of my outlook on life is a complete 360 with all these people in my corner. I don't worry about having too many friends, or being anything I'm not. I know I'm loved today and that makes me love life. It's what they called a safety net in the RDAP program. It's not just for addiction, but simply for mental health and mindset.

Without my safety net, the supportive, healthy circle of people who genuinely care for me today, it is highly unlikely that I would have anywhere near the quality of life I have now. It's more than just a passing or fleeting kind of love that my family and friends show me today. I don't feel worthless and lost. A support system/safety net is a must for the mentally ill.

Maintaining Mental Stability

There are several ways I changed my mindset to be more mentally stable. The first would be to avoid negativity and negative thinking. Negative thinking stops growth, and if you suffer delusions, negativity can bring you places that it's difficult to return from, it's destructive. I tried to improve what I could control on my own, like the way I viewed challenges and the people around me. Whether it was a friend, family member, inmate or prison guard—I started with respect.

I held my tongue when I had something negative to say, or when I didn't have a productive way to say it. I tried to get along with everyone that I could. I used assertive communication instead of aggressive or passive communication. I watched how closely I let people in who were negative. If I decided a person had views and an attitude that did not contribute to positive thinking, I was careful how I interacted with that person.

When you let negative people in, their negativity tends to rub off on you. I do my best not to associate with negativity, and if I must associate with negative people I try not to feed the flames of negativity. Being schizoaffective, negativity is like cancer. If you let it in, it grows and kills you from the inside much quicker than it does with a healthy individual.

Positivity is growth productive instead of growth destructive like negativity, because when I'm positive my world seems like a better place. I think constructively. The voices are less of a nuisance when I maintain a positive mindset. They're still there and they can say some cruel things, but when I'm positive they don't affect me as much. It's easier to use coping skills when you're positive.

Another way I changed my mindset was in deciding that I was going to live my life the right way.

The decision to let go of my past and learn from my mistakes helped me change as a person and become more mentally sound. The voices are good about reminding me of every mistake I've ever made. Sometimes it's random things that I don't think about often; suddenly, there it is—a bad memory for the voices to taunt me with. Using my mistakes as a springboard for learning helps me to not get hung up when the voices want to be cruel about my past. Today, I use those past mistakes and the reminders of them to be a better person.

I also decided to focus on success. Setting goals and working toward them helps me not to regress back into the days of delusion and homelessness. Everyone has ideas about success. I believe that as of this writing I am already a success in many ways. I've come a long way with my illness and the way I cope. I have a business and have been achieving goals or working to achieve them, daily. Success will never cease to be something I strive for. It doesn't stop evolving. I think to be a success and keep being a success, you must move forward and not let your past hold you in one place. I have realized some success and I plan to realize a whole lot more.

I also realized what kind of difference it made in my life to avoid illegal narcotics and people involved with them. I knew a lot of cool people, good people that had drug addictions, or were involved in one way or another with illegal narcotics. My mindset of acceptance of these things has changed. If I could, I would change other people's situations, but I can only control mine. I no longer believe that it's okay to hang around users. The decision was a difficult one for me to make, because my life was infected with the crowds and scenes that these things breed in, for many years. Taking a stance and changing my mindset to not accept the lifestyle and company that will pollute my mental health must be maintained and cared for.

When you're mentally ill and have been a drug addict, removing yourself from the drug life and associations will help you maintain a healthy lifestyle and put you on the road to success. I know it's hard to let go of the people and places where these things breed if they've been part of your life for most of your life, or you've been using them as an escape. The thing is, they aren't an escape they're a trap. There are a lot of sick people caught in the trap and turmoil of the drug life. You must truly want a better life and you must be steadfast in the decision that illegal narcotics are poison and that without them life may not be perfect, but there's no escape from the imperfections of life. Face your problems and do something about them. When we use, most of us are just masking pain. Quit trying to escape the pain. That was my decision and it worked for me. My mindset is that illegal narcotics are poison.

I had to change the mindset that told me that I had to help the world, even when they weren't grateful. The belief that it was my responsibility to pull people out of the ruts they placed themselves in is difficult to move past. The kind of stress I would put myself through to 'save' people was unhealthy. The thing is, you can't save someone who doesn't want to be saved. I have changed my mindset to not constantly seek ways to help people who don't want it. Truthfully, the people you try to help who don't want your help often will resent you. I'm not saying I won't help anyone. I'm a caring person. I believe that if you can help someone you should, but the minute someone shows me they don't want my help, I back off. I don't need that type of stress or negativity.

When I started focusing on forgiveness rather than resentments, my mental state improved tremendously. It's apparent to me now how much I harmed myself and distorted my view of people and the world by harboring resentments. The voices love to feed off hate, and resentment breeds hatred. Thoughts and visions that resentment brings turn into waking nightmares.

Deciding to be a forgiving person was one of the best decisions of my life. I let go of all the weights that drug me to the ground and into the pits of delusion, perversions and despair. When you forgive someone it's more for your health than the person you're forgiving. They may see that you have forgiven them and feel smug, or have an air about them like they've won some epic battle. The beauty is, someone who doesn't know the power of forgiveness may or may not ever realize that the one who forgives wins in the end. They don't realize you won a battle by being forgiving. In the end, it doesn't matter, because it's more about your health than the fight. Letting go of resentments gives you power. The power to move forward and succeed. The power to be healthy and confident.

My mindset changed by becoming a grateful person. I'm grateful for every good thing in my life and even some of the things that are a burden. I'm grateful for the people in my life that stand by me. I'm grateful for every compliment I get, for the shoes on my feet, the truck I drive, the roof over my head.

I'm even grateful to have lived through and experienced my disease and my struggles.

I have a mindset of generosity. I'm generous with my time when I choose to give it. I'm generous with my patience for others, when warranted. I spend hours a week reaching out to incarcerated people. I stop and talk to homeless people. I do my best to be generous with positivity, especially when I know someone needs it.

I have a mindset of responsibility. When it's time to take my medication, I take it. When I have a doctor's appointment, I show up. I'm responsible for my mental health. If I didn't want to be 'saved', no one could save me. It's up to me to take and make the steps necessary to be healthy. I'm responsible for reporting to my probation officer and doing the right thing. I believe responsibility is a stepping stone to good health and a good life.

I have a mindset of accountability. Not just holding myself accountable, but also others. If I'm doing something that's affecting my life in a negative way, I should hold myself accountable for my actions. When someone else is affecting my life in a negative way, I should hold them accountable for their actions. Responsibility and accountability go hand in hand. Holding myself and others accountable helps realize what's good for me and what's not. This way I'm not wasting time making excuses for myself and others, living in delusion.

Honesty is another key element to my improved mental health. Being able to take a close look at my life and being honest about what's not working, what hasn't worked and what is making me sick. This is integral to living a better, saner life. During delusions and hallucinations and drug addiction, you play the blame game. A lot of the time we are less than honest with ourselves when we blame the world and everything in it. Being honest with yourself will help you grow and flourish. If you aren't honest with yourself, you are likely not being responsible or holding accountable the real culprit. Denial of an ailment or the things that ailed you cause disease and insanity to fester unchecked. You are the first line of defense when it comes to a mental disorder. You must live it, so be honest about the things in your life that serve to make you sicker.

Being a more sociable person has helped me change my mindset. I don't try to make friends everywhere I go; in fact, I could probably still be considered antisocial. Today I do try to have conversations with people who approach me. Sometimes I even initiate conversations. It feels good to interact with people in society. There's something about small exchanges that go well that gives me a confidence boost. It's good to get confidence boosts anywhere you can find them when dealing with a disease like schizoaffective disorder. I still have an occasional awkward exchange. The ones that turn out well keep me trying. For me, there's a long way to go on the subject. It means so much to me when someone seems pleased with my company. So, my antisocial mindset is slowly changing, and I like the change. I need more than voices and visions to keep me company. Being mentally ill, I know the difference it makes to have someone to talk to. I'm talking with you through written word, and it feels vindicating.

I changed my mindset of life in general. The way I saw the world around me during times of delusion was through lenses of chaos and war. Everyone was a potential threat. I didn't trust anyone or anything. Lost in hallucination and regressing into delusion on a regular basis, I created the war that hindered my life and success. My view of the world today, with my disease under control, is of a completely different place where peace and success are real possibilities daily.

I enjoy people. Going places excites me. Work is rewarding and therapeutic. Writing has changed my life. The people who have helped me when I was willing to accept help have changed my life. The world is no longer a war zone to me. I'm alive now, more than I may have ever been. Changing my mindset and associations has created a place for me, with the help of others, that I am glad to call my home.

The mindset is arguably the most important part of the mental illness. With a destructive, vengeful, chaotic mindset—how do you calm a disabled psychotic mind? It's impossible. Everything echoes, good and bad. Left to my own thoughts, without pen and pad, with a destructive mind—I will sink into perversion and delusion. There's no way to live a productive life while consumed with mental perversion, delusion, death and voices that echo every negative thing that you can imagine.

When the mind is set toward wholesome, productive, pro-life, pro-social thoughts and ideas— we become stable and happy. The voices echo more of the positive thoughts that we have, the wholesome thoughts, while we become productive and happy. The key to being able to overcome the negativity and turn a life to positivity is rooted in the mindset of the individual. That's how it worked for me. My disease is less of a burden. I'm more in control. All because of the willingness to change the way I think, and to educate myself, and the help of some great people in my life.

I suggest reading *Mindset, The New Psychology of Success*, by Carol S. Dweck, Ph.D. This book helped me immensely. It's a great read for anyone looking to improve the way they think.

9 SPIRITUALITY

When I went off my medication and suffered extreme psychosis in the halfway house, a demonic voice told me that it was my belief in religion through the church that was causing my issues. It was religious superstition. I wanted the hallucinations to stop, and I wanted to be free of the voices, so I renounced my faith in the church silently. Afterward, I told a staff member that I had renounced my faith. She remarked that it was the worst thing anyone had ever said to her. I don't believe that, but I can understand today how I must have sounded to her at the time.

Through everything, even when *The Voice* had told me that I was the Devil, I still believed in Jesus Christ and God the Father. I still pray today, but it's difficult for me to give myself over to faith the way I used to do. It appears a weight was lifted from me when I renounced religion. I still go to church sometimes, but I don't stay long. I pray, because I refuse to let go of God, but I have trouble praying in Jesus' name. Sometimes I still do, because I believe he was a prophet and a good person, the Son of God.

I reach out to know God, but do not want to follow others and hold to a set of beliefs interpreted by someone else. When I hallucinated frequently, Jesus wasn't there. He wasn't ever there. I don't remember seeing him and he never came to help me. *It* was there. *It* was my companion. *It* fought for me. As strange as this is, I know that Jesus was here and that he comforts people, he just never comforted *me*. If he did, I don't remember it.

I've always had issues praying in Jesus' name. Something said to me, *God is with me, why do I have to go through Jesus?* There are people who would quote scriptures and tell me all these reasons they believe I must go through Jesus Christ. I tried to be 'saved' in the way I assume others have, but I don't think I ever was. I tried to think of Jesus as my brother, my savior—supposedly he is the only son of God, born by a virgin mother, but I have other theories that I can't get out of my head.

I have been a Christian. I believe in Christ and that he rose from the grave—not on his own, but by God, our Father. I don't know why I've never seen Jesus, but I've seen demons. I don't know why God makes me able to hear and see all the things that He has allowed me to experience. I want to be a Christian, and I try. I love Jesus, I just don't believe everything I read or hear. If I did I would be in a world of trouble. I hear voices all the time and after a period without medication I start to hallucinate so badly I disconnect with the world.

It wasn't what *The Voice* said, when *It* encouraged me to renounce my faith, that matters. What happened after I let go of religion is that a weight lifted from me, I felt freed. It was my religious superstition I let go of. I thought I was the Devil, and if God liked me, why did he make me sick inside? When I let go of that, I just felt better. Oddly enough, I still value the Bible. I believe the stories about Jesus. I like Christians and I wish I could be a better one. I'm just sick of superstitions and everyone's opinion about this and that to secure my afterlife. I'm focusing on securing a better life while I'm breathing. I'm tired of getting so sick I can't function. I don't need to believe the same as everyone else. I'm learning how to please God and live my life the best I can, any way I can.

Some of the books that helped me a lot were written from a Christian perspective. I don't have to believe the same as everyone else or argue details. I do everything I can to avoid superstition. Religion incites superstition sometimes and I don't like it. Talking religion with people almost always leads to drawn out debates and arguments of who's version is the right version. Religion does some great things and it does some horrible things.

What I like about Christianity is that if you read it right, it's all about love. That's something I can get behind. The stories in the Bible are great lessons. There are people who love the lessons and so do I. The thing is, I don't want to argue. In the end, it's only the end or maybe a new beginning, I don't know. Why say, "We're right and everybody else is going to Hell." Is that love? Or they say, "Do this or that, and you won't get into Heaven." I don't think so. There are a lot of things in this life that result in Heaven or Hell right here on earth—happiness is a state of mind. I choose to focus on that now.

I don't think God hates me. I believe he gets pleasure watching us. I think that making the most of your time here is what God likes. I think that living right and pursuing happiness and love pleases Him. I don't think that after death you get to Heaven's gate and He says, "You believed the wrong religion, you're going to Hell." I could see Him saying, "You're a jerk, go to Hell."

If this upsets you, ask yourself why. I'm willing to bet it goes against your beliefs. The fact is that being schizoaffective and superstitious, thinking I was being judged at every turn by an entity who would make me burn in Hell didn't help my delusions. On the other hand, religion could be a good thing if it doesn't make you fanatical.

I sat in churches many times hallucinating, getting 'saved'. It didn't work. What worked for me was changing my mindset. Although I still like to go to church sometimes, it's not the same. There are great people in every crowd, and I think there's an abundance of great people in the churches. I just don't believe the same way some of them do.

As upsetting as it may seem, no religion is 100% right because even though they're supposed to be teaching 'the word of God', man has written it and is interpreting it. Priests, preachers, teachers, councils structure their churches around their interpretation of God or their holy book. My favorite Christian denomination is Baptist, because that's how I was raised. It's like going home and sitting with extended relatives for a while when I'm around Baptist people. The most frustrating argument from them for me is that they're teaching the 'word of God'. Why does God need you to interpret his word for me?

I think if God wrote any of us a letter, we would be able to understand it. Why else would he write us letters? He supposedly knows us better than we know ourselves, right? He could write a letter knowing what we'd understand. I don't think you need some 'smart' or 'holy' man to read the word of God and tell you what it means. When I picked up the Bible and read it from cover to cover on my own, without someone telling me what they thought every passage meant, I think I understood it better.

The thing is, to be 'saved' you must want to be 'saved', whether in religion or in life in the general sense. Church leaders say, "Believe what I believe and you are guaranteed a place in Heaven." They say, "Do as I tell you and you will have eternal life, follow my doctrine or burn in Hell."

I don't believe it's that simple. Knowing how many religions there are and how different they are from one another; it makes no sense. Basically, if you're born and raised in a certain place and with a certain religion, you will be 'saved'? I don't think so. I'm sure it's all very entertaining to God, but I'm not so easily a sheep. Even though I am a Christian by birth and love the Christian churches, I refuse to follow blindly, but by faith—I trust in God.

There have been many prophets in the past and there're likely many walking amongst us today. People listen to and believe what they want. No one can 'save' someone who doesn't want to be 'saved', and I believe God saves whom he wishes, because God knows what's in our hearts and minds. You can't fool God by following a church, and I don't believe that your church decides who will go to Heaven and who will not. That is up to God. Don't be a jerk and maybe he will let you in his kingdom.

The relief that comes to me as a mental patient from not being held to a church's standard is beneficial in my opinion. My dark thoughts become less disturbing. I have gathered coping methods and lifestyle queues from religious based books. One of my favorites is *The Power of Positive Thinking,* by Norman Vincent Peale. There are some great mental exercises in that book that have stuck with me and help me a great deal; for example, the practice of imagining that you are on a ship in the middle of the ocean and throwing your problems and negativity overboard. I use that every day.

Another great spiritual book which has had a lasting impact on me is *The Purpose Driven Life,* by Rick Warren. This book talks about all types of issues. My favorite parts are about relationships with your family. I have a quote from this book tattooed on my body. Books like this have been beneficial to my mindset in one way or the other.

I may not believe in the same way as some, but I do believe that I am a child of God and no one can take that from me. Following a certain religion and living in a manner that some other man tells me I must live—such things hold no sway over God Almighty and I maintain that my God loves me. We don't have to be blind followers or believe the same as others to be 'saved'.

I'm not debunking anyone's religion individually or at all, really. I think it's important to have a belief system, and if religion helps you, more power to you.

Arguments of faith

You can probably imagine the types of conversations and arguments that I've had about faith and religious superstition. I dissected parts of the Bible and would talk with a friend about religious subjects, and these discussions were often heated ones. Things are not always what they appear to be. In my eyes, it is a flawed position to assume that your understanding and interpretation of truth and religion should be the guideline for everyone else's experience. I like to consider every angle and possibility that I can imagine.

To resist putting my faith in others' interpretations and to voice my thoughts and speculations on subjects that are dear to others can be touchy. There are people who believe so strongly in what they've been taught and told that they become red in the face defending their beliefs. Theoretically, there's nothing wrong with having such strong faith in a subject, if it doesn't foster an unhealthy break with reality or unrealistic expectations of conformity on the part of other people.

They say that, to believe, you must have faith. I have faith in God, but not in religion. There are those who may say, "You have to believe like I believe or you don't have faith." My faith in religion has diminished and all but burnt to cinders. My faith in God has grown stronger than ever from my lack of faith in religion. I believe God is with me and always has been. He gave me *It*. When I walked through hell, God did not abandon me. He gave me an army. He made me a General.

As a direct effect of schizoaffective disorder, I have found strengths within myself that I would not know I possessed otherwise. People say, "You can't really have faith without religion."—I disagree. I began to place my faith in God, rather than in religion, and started seeing my ailment as less of a curse and more of a gift. Granted, it is a gift that must be carefully handled and kept in check; even so, it is a gift from God.

God is the One. He is power and intelligence, my favorite words. I don't need a middle man of any sort to talk to and know Him. I don't deny that there were prophets of God and miracles. I don't deny that there are channels you can go through if you need help communicating. Such people are merely translators to me. God is with me and always will be. In that alone I have faith.

Hebrews 11:6

10 COPING SKILLS

All coping skills begin with a thought process. Schizoaffective disorder can take a patient to some dark places. When I was going through intense hallucinations, I sometimes believed that I somehow *deserved* those awful experiences. Other times, I simply couldn't understand why it was happening. Without proper coping skills, a patient will sink further into delusion and chaos. The mind becomes a battlefield and the experience can be emotionally upsetting when one is losing the mental war. Worse than that is the disorientation of not knowing when you're winning or losing, but being suspended in misery.

The first thing is to grasp what you can of reality. When everything is about as crazy and jumbled as it can get, find an anchor. By *anchor* I mean something tangible. Try looking at the situation as if you were not you at all. Are these things happening? If you're in an advanced state of psychosis, this could be hard to determine. If you need to, ask someone if they can see what you see or hear what you hear. During an episode, the hallucinations appear to be extremely real and colorful. Most of the time, if you ask someone, they will say that they don't hear or see what you are experiencing. You'll wonder whether they are lying. Perhaps they are being made to deny what's happening? This thinking could lead you down darker paths. The important thing is that you're expressing yourself and opening yourself up by reaching out when you ask others to validate what you're experiencing. The coping mechanism is to try to ground yourself in some sort of reality. It's important to get leveled out on medication and never stop grounding yourself in agreeable reality.

Losing touch with reality can happen quickly and aggressively. It's important to get help when you start to lose control, as quickly as possible. Express yourself and tell someone close what's happening with you. Go to the hospital and get medication. Find a way back before you're lost in delusion. Start at the earliest signs.

Another method is to use mental techniques like the one I pulled from *The Power of Positive Thinking* by Norman Vincent Peale. Aids like the ones that Dr. Peale described in that book may help you in discarding negative thoughts and problems that you have no control over. As I've said, I use the methods from this book daily. He basically says to imagine you're on an ocean liner in the middle of the sea and you're putting all your problems and negativity into boxes to throw overboard. Then imagine the ocean swallowing those problems and negativity to such depths that they can never be retrieved. I repeat the phrase, *'Throw that overboard'* in my mind every time I have a thought that doesn't seem quite right.

Think positive thoughts and you will get positive results. This works especially well with proper medication and rest. Positive thoughts breed positivity. One way to have some positive thoughts ready to repeat in your mind is to practice them by writing them down. Positive affirmations will help to change your mindset and make schizophrenia/schizoaffective disorder more manageable. If you suffer, you know (like I do) that the voices repeat things over and over. Drown them out with positive affirmations. The affirmations can be about anything you'd like that makes you feel good inside. Say them in the mirror, in the shower, while you wait at your appointments. I suggest trying to say them in your head as much as possible when in public. Before you know it, some of the voices in your head may get on board with you—train them to voice positive affirmations so that their input is no longer solely negative and disturbing.

Journal daily. If you don't care to journal, write a story, get a pen pal, or simply write down a few of your thoughts and come back to read them later. Catalogue your progress in any way you can. Set your mind loose on the page and see what you can create. It works for me. The voices even help me write. They aren't such a burden when I'm writing. If it works for me, it could work for you, too. I get such pleasure from using my creative faculties. When I write I truly feel like the curse has become a gift.

Reading is another coping mechanism for me. When I'm going through severe psychosis reading can become very difficult, but when I'm level and able to concentrate, reading is a calm and entertaining exercise. Reading fills your head with thoughts and ideas that you wouldn't have otherwise. I enjoy reading both fiction and non-fiction. There are so many good books and you can take something away from everything you read. If you are a solitary person like me, reading can be much more than just educationally beneficial. It's as though the author is an old friend telling you a story. The characters become an extension of yourself. You gain knowledge and wisdom from some books that can change the way you think about the world. You can visit other worlds and be inside the mind of someone else for a short time. Being schizoaffective, reading may be even better, more vivid. I can see the scenes and characters and some of them have stayed with me for years. A few of my favorite books are *On Writing* by Stephen King, *Life Expectancy* by Dean Koontz, *A Painted House* by John Grisham—and there are many others I've enjoyed as well.

Group meetings are also beneficial. When I was practically brain damaged and the voices and visions never gave me a rest, I would go to groups like NA and AA just so that I could sit with others and concentrate on listening to the group talk. I like to look at the person talking and read their lips as they speak. It was another exercise in grounding myself. It was good to sit and listen knowing that the voices I was hearing were real. I enjoy all types of groups. Church was good for this, also.

Listening to music can help when you're not suffering heavy psychosis. I like to listen to music while I write and when I exercise. Most of the time, when I'm writing or reading, instrumental or classical music are my favorites—I like music that doesn't interfere with my thoughts and creative voices when

I'm cranking out text or getting involved in a good book. Other times I listen to all types of music while I pace my room. It's therapeutic. I go places in my mind with some background noise from the tunes. It's like a vacation. Music helps with exercise because I get lost in the moment.

Exercise is good for coping. It gets the blood pumping and is a boost to the self-esteem when a routine is completed. Having a healthy body promotes having a healthy mind. Coming up with exercise routines and completing them are accomplishments. Accomplishments make you feel good. Being schizoaffective, you can use that feeling more than some. Everything that makes you feel good makes you think better and be stronger in who you are.

Opening up to your family and doctors is a good coping method. Really opening up and letting them in on the things you experience. Having someone to discuss your condition with is an important element to maintaining a decent quality of life with schizoaffective disorder. When we hold everything inside, it festers and problems grow out of control when unchecked.

Overall mental health depends on how willing you are to work with the people around you to become stable. With schizoaffective disorder, being unstable is an animal of its own. Finding and implementing coping skills will help aid in recovery and in maintaining a more substantial life. Being sick and unchecked, and neglecting to develop good coping skills, will lead to all kinds of complications, including drug use, criminal activity and behaviors, aggression, homelessness and alienation. No one wants to suffer these things or regress into combat with society if they want a fulfilling life.

Don't let your disorders be an excuse to underachieve. Just because you struggle does not mean you can't succeed. There's too much going on in a schizoaffective mind to let it all go to waste. Remember that the disease does not make you less, it can make you more. Most people with schizophrenia/schizoaffective disorder are highly intelligent. Show yourself and get it under control, you never know where life could take you with the aid of prescription drugs and a few effective coping skills.

I advocate medication because it helps me a lot. I used to be completely against it. I've discovered the benefits of medication and education. The longer you wait or deny yourself the longer it will take to get on track. It took me years to get the combination of medications that works for me today. Trial and error is required but one thing is apparent to me today—it's worth it.

11 MY LIFE AS OF THIS WRITING

Schizoaffective disorder does not hold me back today because I do the right things. I'm more conscious of my mental and physical health now than I've ever been. I take all my medications when I'm supposed to and make all my doctors' appointments on time when possible. I also frequent the gym and I feel well-rounded and healthy.

Since coming home from the halfway house, I've built relationships with my family, probation officer and counselors. A woman who used to write letters to me when I was in prison flew several times from New York to visit me here in Texas. I think that says a lot for me as a person, and for her. She made me feel love again like I hadn't felt in a long time, and in turn made me a better person.

I wake up every day to work and take care of my hygiene. When I go to work outside of my home it always feels like an adventure. I own a small furniture repair business that keeps me fairly busy. I like to work on furniture because it's gratifying when I complete something and the customer is satisfied.

I'm working on getting a second company up and running that will deal with commercial woodwork. Having projects and working for myself is exciting. My father helps me with all of it and if it weren't for him I don't know what I'd do. I try my best to be as self-sufficient as possible, but I do need and accept help and am fortunate enough to have someone in my life who makes a huge effort to help me be successful.

Every day I work on my writing. I write more than anything else I do. It makes me feel good and I get a sense of achievement every time I sit down and inch forward on a writing project. I like to write poetry, short stories, novels and anything else I'm inspired to delve into. Writing letters to people in prison is also therapeutic for me. I've been there and when I feel like I'm making even the smallest difference in someone's life, in a positive way, it helps me also. It's hard to feel worthless when there's someone looking forward to interacting with you. That goes both ways.

Hearing voices is a constant thing, even with medication. It took me a while to realize they weren't going to go away, no matter how many adjustments were made to my dosage. Over the years I've learned that it's a combination of medications and coping skills/methods that work best for me. Today I'm aware that medication will not solve all my problems, but it helps.

My nightmares have turned into agreeable dreams. I still have nightmares, but they aren't constant. I fill my mind with positive thoughts and information that will help me reach my goals. It's like I said before: With schizoaffective disorder the voices repeat things over and over sometimes. The visions form out of predominant thoughts. Hallucinations are manifestations of thoughts and visions. To change all of this starts with the mindset and what you fill your head with. If you seek and find positive things to think about and focus on, the voices, visions and thoughts become beneficial.

Hallucinations will always be the biggest burden when dealing with schizoaffective disorder. When I'm riding alone in my truck, I often see *It* in the seat next to me. There are numerous other hallucinations—on walls; people in the distance. The best way I have of combating the hallucinations is by taking prescription, anti-psychosis pills. Other than taking medication, I simply do not give the hallucinations power. I don't focus on them or try to catch everything in my peripheral vision.

Days go by that I barely have any disturbances in regards to hallucinations. Schizoaffective disorder is a progressive disease, so I do dread the possibility that the medication will stop working for me—or that one day I will be forever lost to the world. I choose not to focus on the fear that I may lose my mind completely. My best defense to the thought of becoming mentally disabled again (or maybe even permanently) is to create goals and keep up with my health the best I can.

My children are a bigger part of my life now than they have been since they were the age of ten. They're adults now, and they make time to call and text me. I live over two hours away from my children, so I relish every opportunity to visit them. A beautiful thing happened on my last birthday! I wasn't expecting company, and my father and I were sitting in the back yard at home, enjoying the weather. He asked me how

I was feeling, and I told him that I was blessed—living at home and feeling healthy—I said that it just couldn't get much better than that.

I was mistaken—no sooner than I had completed my sentence, my daughter walked out of the back door and embraced me, surprising me with a birthday visit. So, things did get better that day in an unexpected way, and so does my life continue to get better as the days pass. My son has two daughters, and my son has come a long way in forgiving me my absence as a father to him. He calls and encourages me to visit my granddaughters. He also tells me he loves me every time we talk or see each other. It means more to me than anything to know that my children love me.

My granddaughters gravitate to me when I visit. They climb all over me and crawl up to curl up next to me. I feel like I have a chance to be a part of their lives and I don't plan on taking that for granted. I will not let my disease get out of hand and lose the connections I have made.

Today, it is more important to me to be free and healthy, mentally and physically, than it has been to me since my children were born. I lost my resolve to be healthy when I was younger and let my mental faculties spiral out of control. Today, I do not have those setbacks.

My disorder was once a thing of shame to me. The people I hung around with glorified drug use, but when I needed mental health help, they saw it as a weakness. "You don't need medication. There's nothing wrong with you."—these are the words of people who truly don't care. I avoid those people today, but not because I care what they think—it's because I *don't* care what they think. I don't need uneducated opinions of people who wouldn't care less if I was sleeping in the gutter.

I don't care about being the cool guy, or the normal guy, or the crazy guy. I do care about being a good son, brother, uncle, father and grandfather. I care about success. I care about my goals. I care about having healthy dreams and relationships. If you're not about that, we probably won't relate. If you are, congratulations, I wish you the best.

At the time of this writing I am sitting in a local coffee shop that I love. It's one of my favorite places to be. I frequent a local gym, where the people seem to like me and I take care of the business of my physical health. Other than those two places, you may find me in my shop working on furniture, on the road to Dallas to work and visit family, or in my room writing a book.

I love my life today. I'm no longer in Hell. People seem to like making my acquaintance, there are people who care for me, and I love and care for them, too. It has been a long and chaotic process to get to where I am today. My mind is a strange thing. So many thoughts come to me each day that would have thrown me off course just a few years ago. I cannot stress enough the power of coping skills and proper medication, people to talk to, and a general focus on health and wellbeing. Being schizoaffective, you need all the help you can get, but you also should want and work toward a better life. No one can control your mind, and even if you can't, you can at least feed it health and let that overactive, complex machine work in your favor.

When I wake up for the day and open a Word

document, I feel refreshed and alive. Writing has changed my life and given me a purpose. Finding something that you enjoy, that gives you a sense of purpose, is important. It could be music or singing or spending time with loved ones. The important thing is that you find reasons to face the day. Schizoaffective disorder could hinder you from enjoyment of life, because of the things you think or believe. Finding positive things to think and do helps you to believe in yourself, and believing in yourself makes nothing impossible.

Driving is a calming activity for me and I do a lot of it. It's not something that you'd want to do while experiencing overwhelming psychosis, but when I'm healthy, I love to drive. In Dallas, it's real cool. I love the city lights.

I like to people watch, too. You can learn some interesting things watching people. Being a writer, it helps that I like to observe people. I come up with fictional characters and their traits by studying people. It's most interesting when 'normal' people are going about their daily activities without seeming to have a care. They do some pretty funny stuff sometimes.

I don't like seeing homeless people. I see them everywhere and I wonder what they went through that landed them in the position they have in life. I know what all I went through and I know that some of them must have experienced some traumatic things to put them on the streets. When I see them standing on the corner holding signs it bothers me. I never did that and I wonder what must be going through their heads to be doing it. I don't understand begging much, but sometimes I give. I wish the world wouldn't pass them by. If it was up to me no one would be homeless. When I see homeless people today, I always try to stop and have a conversation with them if I can. I guess it's my curiosity—and having been there—that makes me like that.

When I can, I take things nice and slow. I don't like to get into a rush. Schizoaffective disorder makes everything in my mind fast pace. I have to consciously slow myself down. It's a funny thing. You wouldn't think I'd get much done taking things slow, but I get more done now than I ever did living in the manic fast lane.

At the time of this writing, I spend most of my days with my father. Without him I would likely be lost. My father and other family members were the ones who kept bringing me to the hospitals and seeking to help me. Today my biggest advocate is my father. He reads all my material and helps me with editing. He helps me keep up with a healthy lifestyle. Most people who meet me today would never know I suffer from mental illness. That is how far I've come with the help of my father. Once again, a support system for someone with schizoaffective disorder is vital. My father helped me edit and publish this very book you're reading.

Today I have a vehement stance against illegal narcotics. They are a nasty poison for someone with schizoaffective disorder and I see them as exactly that, poison. It's critical for me to stay away from anyone who actively uses these poisons. I don't like to associate with those who glorify the use of poisons. It makes me sick. I will not tolerate people using drugs in my presence. If they do, I can assure you I will not keep their company long.

When I'm ready to go to bed at night I take my

meds and usually get a good night's sleep. Although I have difficulties waking and getting myself going in the mornings, I can get things done each day and feel good about myself. If it weren't for the meds, I know my schizoaffective disorder would make my life a living hell.

Goals and achievements

Setting goals and achieving them are a big part of my life now. I write pages and pages of goals. I set daily, weekly, monthly and even yearly goals. I have goals I want to achieve in the next twenty years and some I would like to achieve tomorrow. It helps to be as organized as possible with my mental disorders. It also goes back to having a purpose. You should make purpose for yourself.

Achieving goals gives me a great feeling and I'm sure it could do the same for you. Unless you aim, you will never hit anything, on purpose at least. Making a target and going for it helps you focus, and focus helps you not to get lost in your own mind with nowhere to go. Achieving goals gives me self-confidence and sense of worth. If you set your goals high enough, with a plan of action, even if you don't reach them when you wanted, I bet you come close and that place is nice, too.

Having a plan of action is critical. When you set goals it's best to come up with ways to reach them or you'll go stale in the water. Think about it. You're creative, or you wouldn't be schizophrenic/schizoaffective. Use that overactive mind and come up with interesting ways to get things done. Just remember that organized thing. If you're not doing what you need to be doing to stay healthy you'll lack the focus of someone who does. Being all over the place will get you nowhere quick.

Finally, congratulate yourself. It's a great thing to be health- and goal-oriented. Who doesn't like to achieve things? If you have a condition like schizoaffective disorder, every step in the right direction is a good step and worthy of congratulation. Don't worry about other people congratulating you, congratulate yourself.

The more clearly you think and the more goals you set and the more action you take gets you to a much better place. It's worked for me and I believe it can work for you. If you don't suffer, but know someone who does, encourage them to set goals and follow through. I encourage you to set goals and follow through.

Healthy vs. unhealthy relationships

You can tell healthy and unhealthy relationships apart in several different ways. A relationship is unhealthy if it does not nurture growth. If the person is always suggesting activities that are illegal or bad for your mental or physical health, that person is an unhealthy relation. When the person is concerned with your wellbeing and freedom, that person is a healthy relation.

There are times when you think it's okay to have unhealthy relationships. Maybe it's a girl or guy you're intimate with and things are never on the same page, so you argue and fight. When you are schizoaffective, you don't need this. Even if you love the person, you might be wise to distance yourself. If your schizoaffective disorder has been anything like mine, then your mind takes you to some terrible places. Do you want to wait until things get out of control and that person you loved ends up hating you? I know today, I must break off unhealthy relationships before they are completely destructive.

Another unhealthy relationship is when you have a lover or friend who uses the types of narcotics that make a schizoaffective person deteriorate extremely fast. I had a lot of these friends. When you break away from them, most don't even miss you, so why put yourself in a high-risk situation for someone that would probably ride past you on the curb, and probably wouldn't offer you a plate of food or even attend your funeral. Some of these unhealthy relationships revolve around drugs, so don't be surprised when there's no relationship without dope. They probably call you a bum anyway, put them aside.

A healthy relationship will make you feel wanted and never put you in harm's way. When a person is healthy for you they say, and do things, that are conducive to your success. Most of the time when a relationship is healthy you can hold real conversations that are productive and positive about the life you're living, and where you want to go. Healthy relationships are supportive and nurturing.

You can tell when people are healthy for you by the things they talk about. If a person is all about negativity, drugs or criminal activity—it's apparent they are unhealthy. When a person says hurtful things, or makes you feel 'less than', they are being unhealthy. When a person talks to you about things you can do to better yourself, they are healthy.

It may be difficult to find healthy people to associate with at first. It was for me. Usually because I was unhealthy. Being unhealthy makes it hard for people to relate to you that aren't also unhealthy and living destructive lifestyles. Do everything you can to make yourself as healthy and productive as you can be and—quite naturally—unhealthy people will push away from you and healthy people will gravitate. That's how it worked for me.

There may be those who will despise you; they'll complain how 'you've changed'. Take that as a compliment. It's all about change. Why would you want to stay the same if it's not working for you? Being of strong mind, you will embrace change, and the right people will love you for it.

OPEN LETTERS

Dear Patient,

Hey, what's up? I sat down to write this book for a lot of personal reasons and hoped that maybe my life and situations could help you understand yours a little better. No one asks to be afflicted with a mental disorder and I know how tough it is. Let me tell you, when you think it's the end, it's not.

There were many times I thought of suicide to make it all stop. I know how sick you can get and I understand. I'd like to tell you not to give up. I want you to know that things get better. Try not to think of the world and everyone in it as your enemies. There are a lot of good people here.

I used to hate taking medications. I know how it can make you feel weak. I know it's difficult to keep up with and you get tired of people asking you if you've been taking them. Sometimes it's difficult to understand that those people are looking out for your best interest, and I get that. I'm telling you something real when I say not to let go of those people. If you have someone in your life right now concerned with your health, you're fortunate. Some people don't have that. I know there have been times when I didn't.

I want to tell you not to give up. Don't ever give up. Don't give into the sickness. There is no cure, but you can find comfort. It starts with the way you think. Change is difficult. It was hard for me to change. You have to start really seeing things how they are before you can change. There's a place we go in delusion that I know well. It's called denial. We deny the things that are killing us, making us sicker.

I challenge you to stop denying that you're sick and need help. The longer you wait to acknowledge the things that are dragging you down, the longer it will take to heal. Don't put it off. Change your thinking and lifestyle to promote good health and see and feel the difference. Become obsessed with success.

Are you living on the streets? I know you don't want to stay there. If you don't start concentrating on your mental health, how do you plan to rise above the ashes? I'm here to tell you that things get better and with the right mindset, you can achieve anything.

Take care,
John U. Gunter

Dear Family Member,

Hey, I want to let you know how valuable you are. All those times you made an effort. All the times you will make an effort. That's priceless. Without people like you the world would be a much darker place. Don't be too concerned if your loved one doesn't seem to come to their senses and sanity like you would like. Keep being there and in the end, they will be more grateful than you could imagine, if he or she is anything like me.

It was people like you who made me the person I am today. I've gone through so many phases and done so many things. Believe me when I tell you that you make a difference. Family members who care matter more than anything when it comes to mental health and recovery.

Have patience and understanding. Most of the time when we're going through mental dilemmas we don't know which way to turn. We might show up on your doorstep dirty and hungry. Thank you for every time you took someone like me in. It's hard to show gratitude when your delusional, but let me tell you what a great kindness you show when you attempt to help someone in poor condition.

You are an encouragement and a light in the darkness that clouds the minds of the mentally unstable. I'm sorry If I ever scared you. If you can't understand what I'm telling you here, I want to make it perfectly clear. I love you.

Thank you,
John U. Gunter

Dear Caregiver,

It's hard to express my gratitude to you, because I could never say enough to tell you how much your work means to people like me. Dropped at your doorstep, you didn't turn me away. You took me in time and again, attempting to fix me. Fix me is the term, because for years I was broken, a shell of a man. You brought me back from the depths of despair.

Through my hospitalizations there were many caring people. You didn't give up on me. You worked with me until something worked. There are many of you, and everywhere I went there was someone like you, helping to guide me through the fog. I want to thank you for everything you do. I want to tell you what a difference you make.

I know it's hard. There are so many that need help. So many that are poisoning themselves, or refuse to do what they need to so that they can get better. I was one of those patients. Here I am. My success is yours. I hope this book helps people the way you have helped me. You are heroes and heroines.

Forever grateful,
John U. Gunter

MY POETRY

Writing poetry has been helpful to me for many years. I benefit from writing in general, but poetry has a special place for me. Using it to express my pleasures and pains awakens feelings inside me that help me understand myself. I am including several poems in this book. I hope you read and enjoy them.

Maybe they will inspire you to write some of your own or give you food for thought. I'm going to include several types and they are all special to me. Most of them revolve around my mental health issues. There's something about exercising the darkness within and expelling it properly that gives me joy.

To live a happy life, you should figure out ways to satisfy your heart's desires and express yourself. This is one of my vehicles of expression and I recommend it to anyone. It's a great place to start.

HELLO AGAIN

Hello. I haven't looked at you in a while,
I almost forgot what you looked like.
Sometimes I think you haven't been here lately,
But I know you're always here.

You're a strange one,
You follow me everywhere,
Telling me weird things.
Things no one else tells me.

No one else,
You aren't a person.
Not really.
You're just my cruel counterpart.
Well, you're not always cruel,
But you've been crueler,
Than any mortal person I have ever known.

I feel like I'm talking to myself,
But I know you're real in some sense.
I see you in the mirror,
And in the corner of my eye.

I can only look you in the eyes through my own.
You have always been there.

BROKEN

Down in a hole,
I claw to find a way out,
I'm not alone here,
But sanity has all but left me.
Who is it that speaks to me,
My wings are torn and tattered.

You look down on me,
I feel your judgments,
The smirk on your face,
Tells me you don't understand.
I'm broken but not dead.

A light is there,
But I'm in no tunnel,
I dug this hole,
And now I search for a way out,
My fingers are bloody,
My fingernails are full of mud.

Won't you reach in and give me a hand?
I will be free,
And I'll prosper,
But I must escape this pit.

READING BETWEEN THE LINES

Can you see like me?
Read me close and understand,
Under the surface,
There's an animal.
I'm no longer as wild.

When you lose touch with reality,
You see more than you choose.
It's not as simple as closing your eyes,
The visions are there,
And reality is not always your friend.
It's just a place to start.

WORLD OF WORDS

My eyes are open,
My troubles are real,
Life is a token,
That I began to steal.

I took the wrong road,
Lived behind wire and locked gates,
I stuck to a code,
And accepted my fate.

I realized something vital,
While in my captors' grasp,
I have a talent for title.
For what you might ask?

The written word is my gift,
Long after I'm gone it will exist,
In life gears shift,
Our plots have turns and twists.

BIRDS FLY

I'm not getting any younger,
My kids are getting older,
Away from home so long,
My time is now spent sober.

My mind is sometimes berserk,
My sanity wearing thin,
They had me on lock and key,
Inside the Federal Pen.

Freedom churned inside my mind,
Couldn't let that place win,
If I let it take control,
That would have been the end.

There's life beyond those walls,
That's where I wanted to be—
There are places to go,
Plenty of things to see.

If I can have it my way,
I won't ever go back—
I'll be in the free,
Making my papers stack.

CURVE BALLS

I write to think free,
I write just being me,
I get peace of mind,
When I write these rhymes.

I pen and type words,
Using adjectives, nouns and verbs—
Life throws me curves,
That's why I'm disturbed.

I've gone through Hell before—
My head drops to the floor,
I ask the ONE above,
To see me to the shore.

I have what I need,
No more need to Speed—
I'd like to write material,
That people stop to read.

It's all in progress and plan,
To ONE DAY acquire the land,
For the better I make a Stand,
EVERYTHING is in GOD's hands.

ENIGMA

I've been locked away in a hole—
Breaking the fragments of time,
Scattered into a million pieces.
To my agony they were all blind.

I'm a difficult person to know,
I have a chaotic mind—
Because every day I live,
With a Cruel Counterpart, inside.

I try to see the Good in People,
And with most I get along.
The Turbulence and Turmoil—
Comes from living my life so wrong.

There's Pressure Building to a Bursting point,
Produced by Deranged thoughts.
I speak to Angels and Demons at night—
And Dream of Twisted Plots.

AMID RUIN

Havoc wrecked my world,
To the Heavens I cursed,
Lost in a maze of hysteria—
It was not clear who I was.

Mortal, though I may be,
I traveled many streets—
And claimed the rose for myself,
Although it cannot be seen.

Through walls of defeat,
I have broken free—
With a single name coveted,
Never to be mine again.

The disastrous depths of despair,
Leaves ruined, some who pass there—
My Soul, it has not captured.
I am free—
Because I believe myself to be.

JUST PURSUE IT

Making the same mistakes,
Always makes me crazy,
I'll do what it takes,
And try not to be lazy.

The times are changing,
And so is my mind,
Good vibes I'm arranging,
Doing my best to be kind.

Now I realize,
It's better to take it slow,
Working, in my eyes,
Is the way to go.

I think, pursue it,
Is the phrase to go by.
I must pursue it,
To say more than—I tried.

MENTAL SOUP

Just need a little polish—
On this complex—living machine.
It could have been Demolished,
That's such an ugly scene.

How did it pull through?
That's the question asked.
A new DESTINY it drew,
Leaving behind the past.

It remembers,
Memories pushed to the back.
From the fire are embers,
On the conscience, they attack.

Since that cannot be changed—
It's best to move on.
Take care of your brains,
They are what you have, LIFE LONG.

MIDNIGHT

Just a tiny glimpse inside,
A hectic and Diabolical mind.
Over mountains of thoughts I've spun—
Through Madness I've overcome and climbed.

Reality is a Dirty bubble,
And time is bursting the seam.
As the chaos grows uncontrollable—
The twilight's darkness drawing me in like a dream.

I fixate on what could be—
Losing my place with what has been.
Rolling around in the filth of it all—
Buried in deeds of Devilish Bastard sin.

As the clock tolls twelve,
I rummage through this Hell—
Always attempting to find my way,
Until the time comes I no longer dwell.

JOHN U. GUNTER

PIECES OF MY MIND

I like getting things done,
It's a plus to have fun—
No more life on the run,
No more smoking guns.

Up against problems happens,
Some experience emotional high-jacking,
That's when things get crazy,
This life has all the trappings.

Sometimes it's best to move around,
Peace—may occasionally be found,
Don't get ran into the ground—
Or end up in the pound.

Most have roamed astray,
Wandering through the days—
It's not always time to play,
But Everyone has their ways.

I get by on my faith in God,
I've left disaster in my wake,
Inside I feel familiar aches,
Some things aren't easy to shake.

THE ATMOSPHERE

I wander through galaxies in my mind,
Worlds spin and collide with a masterful beauty.
I've been here from existence,
In a space, small and also limitless.

The destruction of everything that has passed,
Mixed with infinite creation.
It doesn't seem like there will be an end,
There will always be something in the distance.

Minutes, hours, days and months,
These things have little meaning in eternity,
Time is infinite—
Even if there is no witness.

Doing what we can with what we have,
Making progress to nothingness in 'time'—
Everything will be as it will be,
And I will be the room.

I'm disturbed and at times distant,
Because I find peace in seclusion—
But everyone needs someone, eventually.
Compatibility could be an illusion.

Ambience of relevance in my atmosphere.

POST TRAUMATIC

Thoughts trickle and take Toll—
Another day whisking away, beginning to grow Old.
Everything is sure to pass—
Into the wind I Scold.

Understand I am a troubled soul—
Tortured by what has been.
I try to lay my worries to rest,
And I look for peace from within.

I realize fortune in the smallest things,
Like a soft place to lay my head.
I'm not concerned with trivial beings,
Like monsters under my bed.

The horror of Suffering Inhumanities—
Seeping through these Blood-filled veins.
The mirror sometimes haunts me.
My memories are set and Ingrained.

THE BOOK OF TRIALS

There's a story inside my head—
I would like it to be told before I'm dead.
Chaotically churning, out of control,
I begin with the pen, to say what needs to be told.

Starting from the beginning, with birth—
This tale, with time, grows in mirth.
Troubles, sorrows and sickness fill the blank page,
Speaking of a somber soul, consumed with rage.

Parties, pitfalls and perversions—to dine,
Yes, an overflowing occurrence in the delicate web.
The tale of a yelling madman, lost in his mind—
Of which, he searches for redemption.

Not a flowery prose, but a furnace—
Any soul whom lived this, would surely be scorched.
Intricate insanity, teetering the edge of twisted,
And delusions of paradise, torched.

TIME IS SLIPPING

I sit alone and think,
Losing track of what has me on the brink,
Into these thoughts I sink.

The days pass slowly by—
To maintain my sanity, I try.
There are seldom people surrounding.
In my head voices pounding.

Now the sounds are resounding—
All my experiences are compounding.
It's driving me mad,
But this existence isn't all bad.

Then again, I do need space,
Waiting seems such a waste,
Waiting is the challenge—
Challenge is my life.

MY SCHIZOPHRENIA

SUGGESTED READING

Fiction:

Grisham, John. *A Painted House,* Doubleday 2001

Gunter, John U. *Drugs, Sex & Death Toll,* Self-published 2016, available at Amazon.com

Koontz, Dean. *Life Expectancy*, Bantam Books 2012

Non-fiction:

Dweck, Carol S., Ph.D. *Mindset: The New Psychology of Success*, Random House 2007

King, Stephen. *On Writing*, Scribner, 10th Anniversary Edition 2010

Peale, Norman Vincent. *The Power of Positive Thinking*, Touchstone 2003

Van Ekeren, Glenn. *The Speakers Sourcebook*, Prentiss Hall Press 1994

Warren, Rick. *The Purpose Driven Life*, Zondervan 2002

I absolutely love these books and authors, and yes, I love myself..

ABOUT THE AUTHOR

JOHN U. GUNTER is the author of unique short stories and novels, many of which are drawn from or largely colored by an early life of crime and a continuing struggle with schizo-affective disorder. John lives in Texas where he writes stories and works to develop local businesses.

MY SCHIZOPHRENIA